To Bridget
Hope y
He

Best wishes

"ATTENTION!!
The SECRET to YOU playing
GREAT golf"

by

Karl Morris

"ATTENTION!! The SECRET to YOU playing GREAT golf"

by

Karl Morris

ISBN: 978-1-905006-38-0

Published by The London Press.

CONTENTS

the mind factor

ACKNOWLEDGEMENTS

My special thanks go to my wife, Nadine, for making all of this possible with her patience, understanding and attention to detail and in general having superior ability in the numerous areas that I am sadly lacking.

Many people have helped me along the way, some know that they have, others don't. For the ones that do know, I have never taken enough time letting you know how much your friendship and help has meant to me over the years.

Brian & Gerry Connor, Scott Connor, Adrian Fryer, Andrew Stevenson, John Andrew, Mike Yorke, Kevin Healey, Tony Wrighton, Rob Woodgate, Duncan Lennard, David Hares, Kristian Baker, Joe Sillett, Alan Kelly, you are all the best of people.

To all of the 500 or so **MIND FACTOR** coaches who have taken the **MIND FACTOR** course with me over the years, I wish I could see you all again at some point. The week we spent together was brief but, for me, special. I thank you for your contribution which means so much.

To Duncan Lennard, my good friend and "man of letters", who knocked a very rough draft into a readable form.

Geniuses such as Philip Zimbardo, James Pennebaker, Mike Hebron, Richard Bandler, Timothy Wilson, Roy Baumeister, Kevin Hogan, Joan Vickers, Debbie Crews, Sian Beilock, Timothy Gallwey, Michael Hall and Trevor Sylvestor.

To some of the great players I have been fortunate to work with from the world of golf. The likes of Graeme McDowell, Darren Clarke, Lee Westwood, Paul McGinley, Louis Oosthuizen, Alison Nicholas, Karen Stupples to name a few and the many others who I have attempted to help at some point but who helped me learn far more for myself and about myself.

the mind factor

From other sports it was a "summers dream" to be involved with Michael Vaughan, the England cricket captain during the greatest of all Ashes series in 2005 and, more recently, my thanks go out to Paul Anderson and Nathan Brown who both had the willingness and open mind to allow me to be involved in the wonderful, tough, brutal and honest world of Rugby League.

Lastly, but most importantly, to Gwynne and Margaret Morris, Mum and Dad. Sadly, Dad long since passed away but, hopefully, some of the things that I have been involved with would have brought a smile to his face.

the mind factor

ABOUT KARL MORRIS

Karl Morris is one of Europe's leading **PERFORMANCE COACHES**, delivering practical methods of peak performance and goal achievement to a range of clients across sports and business.

From the world of golf, he has worked with players such as British Open Champions, Louis Oosthuizen and Darren Clarke, former World Number one Lee Westwood, US Open Champion Graeme McDowell, Masters Champion Charl Schwartzel, Dunhill Links Champion Michael Hoey, Ryder Cup legend Paul McGinley, Jamie Donaldson, Richard Sterne, Richard Finch, US Open Champion Alison Nicholas, British Ladies Open Champion Karen Stupples, Jodi Ewart, Lisa Hall and Trish Johnson.

He has presented **MIND FACTOR** seminars all over the world to the PGA of Great Britain, Australian PGA, South African PGA, Italian PGA, Belgian PGA, German PGA, Swiss PGA, Swedish PGA and the Dutch PGA

Also, working with top class amateurs, he has worked with numerous Walker Cup and Curtis Cup players. He has presented to the Scottish Golf Union, the Welsh Golf Union and the Golfing Union of Ireland.

From other sports he has worked with Ashes winning Captain Michael Vaughan, presented seminars to Premiership Football including Manchester United and, most recently, from the world of Rugby League Huddersfield Giants who in 2013 won the league leaders trophy for the first time in over 80 years.

PROLOGUE

This book is my attempt to share with you some of the thoughts and ideas that I have found to be useful over the years in my coaching. I do not present this to you as an academic or with a wall full of educational certificates. From a conventional educational perspective, I have no validity whatsoever. However, I do come from a position of being involved at the "coal face" of coaching, dealing with human beings in the real world for the best part of thirty years and, I am proud to say, that I have been a member of the PGA of Great Britain for the same length of time.

Over that time, I have been fortunate to work with some of the world's very best players from the PGA Tour, European Tour, LPGA Tour and European Ladies Tour. I have presented the concepts of the **MIND FACTOR** to the PGA's of Great Britain, Australia, South Africa, Germany, Canada, Italy, Holland, Belgium and Switzerland. I have taught the annual **MIND FACTOR** Coach Certification course for 10 years.

Although I am not an academic, many of the ideas you will find in this book are based on the tireless work of people in the scientific and academic communities. We are immensely fortunate to be living in an age where we understand so much more about the human brain and how it functions. The really exciting part is, we are still at first base in terms of what we **WILL** discover in the future. The more we can understand the brain, the more we can learn about the challenges that golf provides us and how best to set course on a programme of improvement. One of the most exciting discoveries the neuro-scientific community has provided us with is the conformation that with the right kind of training, we can literally re-wire our brain and establish new patterns of behaviour and responses. We do not need to be the victim of a pre-determined future.

the mind factor

I personally spent far too long thinking that being a great golfer was all about building a great swing. I also spent far too long thinking it was "all in the mind" when I now firmly believe being the best golfer you can be, involves a blend of learning how to swing the club more efficiently whilst, at the same time, understanding how to think better and control your emotions out in that most unique of environments called a golf course.

I am not for one minute saying I have all of the answers to this immensely rewarding but frustrating game. Anyone who says that is a fool. But, I do hope I am at least going to ask you some different questions during our time together, which will allow you to think about your game in a different way. One thing I do know is that, as human beings, we all like the **IDEA** of change but the **APPLICA-TION** to change is a different matter. My hope would be you would read this book with an open mind and pick out the ideas, tools and techniques you personally find useful. Put your attention on those ideas and make a commitment to implement the change. The time we are about to spend together will allow me to share with you those ideas. I firmly believe what I am about to discuss with you **WILL** make a difference to your experience of the game of golf. If nothing else, when you have read the book and you have implemented some of the ideas, if you can then tell me that your experience of the game of golf is an enjoyable one, I would hope you would deem our time together as being worthwhile.

"He has helped me through some difficult times in my life. He was a major factor on and off the course for four or five years, giving me a basic understanding of how I should work as both a player and a person. I understand much more about myself now, my reactions to myself, my moods. We all know that golf can drive you mad at times and Karl has helped me deal with a **LOT** of things".

GRAEME MCDOWELL
2010 US OPEN CHAMPION AND RYDER CUP HERO

the mind factor

"Working with Karl has been tremendous. He gave me a very clear understanding of how important my routines were on each and every shot. The last round at St Andrews summed up all of the work perfectly".

LOUIS OOSTHUIZEN, 2010 OPEN CHAMPION

ATTENTION!! The SECRET to YOU playing GREAT golf

"I have worked with Karl for over six years and my game
has always benefitted immensely from his input.
I'd recommend he can do the same for you and help
your game tremendously".

DARREN CLARKE, 2011 OPEN CHAMPION

the mind factor

INTRODUCTION
THE POWER OF FOCUSED ATTENTION

The American golfer Raymond Floyd once opined that golf is so-called because "all the other four-letter words were taken". Ever since the game was invented, frustration has never been far away. But my research into the game as a mind and performance coach has clearly shown me one thing – that much of this frustration stems from the rigid and often inflexible approach we have traditionally adopted to tackle the game. Often, a fresh perspective is all that is needed to defeat a stubborn problem – and that is exactly what this book will give you.

The concepts detailed in this book will help you look at your own game in a slightly different way – a way that will reveal to you what you are *truly* capable of experiencing with this wonderful game of golf, and will set you on the correct path to achieve it.

Perhaps you will even begin to discover what golf may be able to teach you in other areas of your life. Not for one minute am I saying I have all of the answers here, but hopefully as we go through the pages of this book, you will see I am at least asking some *different* questions.

Asking different questions is a theme central to this book – and one that underpins my key strategy of working on your game from a fresh perspective. I remember once hearing somebody say: "The quality of your life will be determined by the quality of your questions." From initially not understanding the gravity and importance of this statement, I am, as you will find in this book, convinced this single statement is possibly *the* most important concept you will ever hear. I don't, as you will discover, believe in positive thinking as it is currently peddled by the media and various mind gurus; but I passionately believe in the power of *quality* questions.

Why? Because quality questions focus one of your most precious commodities: your *attention*.

As we will see, your success or failure – in golf and life – will depend to a very large degree on where you place your attention. In very simple terms your attention will either be on something useful to what you are aiming to achieve, or something that isn't. I am hoping that as your eyes fall across the words on this page of the book, your attention is currently on what you are reading. If it is, then you will more than likely gain something from the words you read. However, your attention could be on what you need to do later, on how you are going to feed yourself soon or even what the other people in the room are thinking about you, sat here reading a golf book. As you read those last statements, you may even have found your attention wandering to the very things I mentioned. Sorry about that. But it does just highlight how fragile and temporary our attention can be.

So, a major part of our journey will be to understand and apply the principle of focused attention. You will learn how quality questions can be one of your greatest assets in bringing your attention to a place that is useful and productive. When you have the capability to *direct* your attention, you begin to take control of your world as opposed to the world controlling you.

This has never been a more important ability to possess. In the modern world we inhabit, it would seem that almost every minute of every day, there are a combination of factors and situations which are trying to steal our attention. Look at the incredible way people become "addicted" to social media, or to the constant stream of sound bites and calls-to-action which inhibit and restrict our capability to just be "here and now", with our attention where we want it.

the mind factor

Is it any wonder then that when we get out onto the golf course we struggle to play a game which positively insists on your being attentive to what is going on, right here and now, in this moment, playing this unique shot you will *never* be confronted with again? To be absorbed in the task at hand is, in essence, what the game of golf is about. It is a game where you *never* get to play the same shot twice. It is a random game giving you a puzzle to solve on each and every unique shot. To solve the puzzle, the brain needs to be engaged in the puzzle and your precious attention needs to be with you to solve it.

The problem as I see it with so many golfers, from the very highest level to club players, is they do next-to-nothing to *train* their attention to be in the right place for golf. Believe me, standing on the range bashing ball after ball may (although I doubt it) do something to improve your golf swing, but it does *nothing* to train your attention for the environment called a golf course.

So, asking different questions is vital. But as a second example of fresh perspective, consider the quest for the perfect golf swing. We have been brought up to believe in the holy grail of a consistent swing, a repeatable action that will not let you down. Yet, as we will discover during our journey together, your brain will *never* allow you to have a golf swing which is totally consistent. It may permit you to get very close, but it will never let you *"code"* a movement in your system that is totally reliable. All of this I will explain… plus the science which goes with it.

I have seen countless golf careers ruined by the desperate search for a perfect swing. Yet, in my opinion, most golfers are looking for consistency in *totally* the wrong place! The good news is, I firmly believe there *is* an area you can work on to *develop* real consistency; and when you do, you will become the golfer you are truly capable of being. All it takes is a shift in perspective – and my concept of the Three Phases of Golf will give you exactly that.

Over and over again, I have seen many golfers who have under-achieved with their game. So it is my sincere wish after you read this book, you will set off on a journey of discovery, which will reveal the golfer inside you, – one who will surprise and delight you in the future.

Our journey may be a bit bumpy at times – some of your oldest and most cherished beliefs maybe challenged – but I promise you, if you do hang in there with me, you will begin to play the game in a far more effective and fulfilling way. What you are about to read has been tested and proven to be effective at all levels of the game, from major winners to rank beginners. Most of the ideas you read will be backed by the tireless research of others and, I hope the way I have presented my ideas, will do those people justice.

Let's begin our trip...

CHAPTER 1

HOW TO LEARN THE GOLF SWING

Let's get one thing straight from the start: golf is *not* all in the mind! If you have a dreadful golf swing and a great mind, you will still hit plenty of bad shots. You may feel better about it than most folk, but you will still play some lousy golf.

This is why this book has two distinct goals: not just to help you build a set of tools which will help you control yourself better out on the course; but also to show you how to use your brain to gain a better golf swing.

The really good news about golf is there are only *two* things you need to control to become proficient at the game.

1. The ball
2. Yourself!

The not-so-good news is that because most people get so completely off track in trying to control the ball, they spend virtually no time whatsoever working on the second aspect – controlling themselves.

It's no wonder so many golfers get so bogged down with trying to control the ball. It really is absolutely crazy how so much is written about what to do with a golf club… and yet so little is mentioned in how to apply all this knowledge.

I have been to numerous conferences where golf coaches have analysed and debated, in minute detail, the "ideal" motion of the golf swing. Tiger says "do this", Ernie says "do that" and Phil says "try something else". Yet, what use is *any* of that if we don't first understand *how* we learn – how we take that technical information and turn it into actual movement? It really is a case of the cart before the horse.

I am not going to go into what you should do with a golf club in terms of your swing. For that you need the assistance of a good PGA professional you can trust. Rather, I am going to work with you on *how you can learn* to swing the club better. We need to learn how to build an environment that allows us not only to work on our swing but, more importantly, to take that learning and apply it successfully in that most unique of environments, the golf course itself.

In this, we are indeed fortunate that we can draw on so much recent, inspired research that has explored how our brain learns movement skills. Today, more than ever, we know how to utilise the genius of our brain as opposed to having it work against us.

"IMPROVISERS BY DEFAULT"

Take for example the notion of "muscle memory". Many of us were fed this "wisdom" from a young age. I for one can look back on the days where I took that nugget of information literally and tried to beat my muscles into submission by the number of balls I hit, all in the anticipation that my muscles would *"memorise"* the golf swing and it would never again break down. As it turns out, I needn't have bothered. My efforts were destined to fail.

Professor Krishna Shenoy of Stanford University set out to discover why we all seem to be so inconsistent with actions like golf swings, free throws, pitching and tennis serves. His study concluded that:

The main reason you can't move the same way each and every time, such as swinging a golf club, is that your brain can't plan the swing the same way each time. It is as if each time the brain tries to solve the problem of planning how to move, it does it anew. Practice and training can help the brain solve the problem more capably but people and other primates simply aren't wired for consistency like computers or machines. Instead, people seem to be improvisers by default.

The main conclusion of the study by Shenoy is that because the vast majority of situations requiring significant movement are novel, our brain looks to adapt movement patterns, rather than repeat them. Because of this, we will never be able to "hardwire" a movement in its entirety.

This is an evolutionary survival mechanism, known as Dynamic Systems Theory. Predators never get the chance to catch and kill prey in exactly the same fashion and in exactly the same conditions. So, part of our evolution and survival has depended on a brain remaining flexible to the ever-changing environment.

Getting back to golf, we have nevertheless been sold the idea we can *perfect* our swing so it won't let us down. We then practise that swing in a rigid and structured environment called a practice ground or driving range; and then we attempt to take that perfect model out into an ever-changing, flexible and dynamic environment called a golf course. Is it any wonder so many golfers become totally disillusioned by their inability to transfer their practice game onto the course?

When we look at the research and the way our brain works, we begin to understand why it is such a fallacy to consider we can hone a perfect swing. The biggest lunacy, however, is that after playing poorly on the course, where do we go to fix our game? You guessed it... the practice ground! Here we very quickly hit it well again, head back to the course, and of course play badly again. So, back to the range...

Crazy!

I have often found it amusing talking to elite athletes from other sports. They just cannot understand the collective madness we embrace in the game of golf. A snooker player does most of his practice on a snooker table; a squash player on the squash court; a footballer on a football pitch; yet; the golfer spends an inordinate amount of time on a range – which is *not* golf.

I'm quite aware that telling you your brain does not want you to groove a repeatable swing might not be what you want to hear. But here's the curious thing. Time and again, I have found that when a golfer accepts he will never *"get"* the golf swing – that it's a work in progress that will always come and go – he then sets himself truly free to *play* the game. He suddenly finds himself aligned with the vagaries and inconsistency the game throws at us, and so more able to deal with them; and he begins to find a way to get the ball around the course in the fewest number of shots possible. That sounds a lot like the true nature of golf to me.

It sounds very negative to say we will never have a consistent swing but the paradox is, when we accept this indisputable fact, we become able to better deal with the game itself. As I will explain, it is the ability to play the game of golf – as opposed to just playing the game of "golf swing" – that so many have failed to do.

Please do not confuse what I am saying here as being "anti-swing". I firmly believe in good mechanics and in building the best motion possible, but simply with the understanding your swing will never be completely consistent. This is just one of fresh perspectives I urge you to adopt when learning the game. As we will discover later in this book, there are certain aspects of the game of golf in which we can be *incredibly* consistent; but the swing is not one of them. Once you accept that, the game can become fun again.

LEARNING BETTER MOTION

So let us now look at what we *can* do to build up our skills and develop a swing that is as functional as humanly possible.

The motion of the golf swing, or any motion for that matter, is controlled by "maps" in our brain. These maps are essentially neural connections that direct our muscles in what we want to achieve.

the mind factor

The critical aspect in building a rich map is how we practise our motion; it is not the number of shots we hit but the quality of our *attention* as we are hitting them. The "A" word again! What we pay attention to when we practise is critical to our skill acquisition and development.

Now, if you look at the standard golf lesson that has been given over the past fifty years, you will see a pretty familiar pattern. The pro watches a few shots, leans masterfully on his 7-iron, nods his head a few times, shakes his head a few times. Then he begins to explain what is *wrong* with your swing. Maybe he shows you a video of someone doing what he thinks you *should* be doing. Then he gets you to *think* about your wrists, your shoulders, your knees or whatever body part he deems to be causing the biggest problem with your errant shots.

Once you have been given this "instruction", you are then told to go away and practise this until it becomes automatic. So, you go away and stand on your range and you put your attention on the body part the pro has suggested is causing all of the problems. You begin to hit some shots. It is a bit rusty at first, but you hang in there and start to feel a bit better. You commit to repeating this process a few times before you go onto the course. Having got it "right" on the range, you then take your new swing to the course and, with your attention still on those body parts, you attempt to send your golf ball towards a target. And the results? Probably, if you are like millions of golfers who have gone through this process, not too good! You stick with it but it seems to get worse and worse. Good on the range perhaps, but not so good on the course.

This was a procedure I went through myself countless times as a player and it is the number one complaint I hear from most golfers, from major winners to high handicappers. Yet, by and large, this is what the golf industry keeps us doing... and then wonders why people give up the game in their droves!

So, it would seem that placing our attention on body parts in the golf swing is not proving too efficient for many people. We have known this for a long time anecdotally, but now it seems science is again able to help us understand a little more about why this way of doing things is so unproductive.

INTERNAL FOCUS V EXTERNAL FOCUS

Gabriele Wulf from the University of Las Vegas has spent her academic life studying how we learn movement skills – how we would learn to ski, how we would learn to play basketball and, of course, how we would learn to play golf. The main thrust of her work is that attention – and where we place it – is critical to learning.

Her book *Attention and Motor Skill Learning* is an absolute must for anyone interested in how people learn movement skills. In it, she explains what she terms Internal Focus of Attention and External Focus of Attention. If you are focusing internally, you would have your attention on your body parts and be telling yourself how to move your body through space. If your attention is external, it would be more on the *effect* of the movement. In golfing terms, an external focus would be the motion of the club, or the flight of the ball.

Dr Wulf asked novice golfers to pitch balls with a 9-iron to a 15ft circle. One third of the group was provided with internal focus cues by an instructor. These were based on hand-and-arm movement. Another third of the group was given only external cues (swing the club in a pendulum fashion); the remaining third was given no cues at all. Points were awarded based on how close each golfer landed balls to the target. The results showed that the use of external swing cues increased skill learning by approximately 33%. Golfers who tried to learn the game without any instruction at all fared just as well as those who relied solely on internal swing thoughts.

When I first saw this research, which Dr Wulf has replicated in other learning environments, I was blown away by its importance to the game of golf. A 33% improvement on learning and retention is a staggering amount. But for me, the part of the research we most need to heed is the revelation that golfers who try to learn without *any* instruction fared just as well as those golfers given an internal focus of attention. Does this not reflect an awful lot of what we instinctively already know? Putting your attention on what your body is doing is, for many people, very counterproductive.

Dr Wulf has gone on record as saying that in her 25 years of research, she has seen very little evidence of internal focus being effective in learning a motor skill like golf. Yet, for the past 50 years at least, it would seem this has been the way that golf has been taught!

THE NINE SHOTS

So what does all this mean for your game?

My suggestion would be that if you feel you have stalled in trying to improve how you swing a golf club, then you should really consider where you are placing your attention. If you have spent 10 years working on moving your body in a certain way with little or no progress, then maybe it is time to shift your focus externally.

My suggestion would be to become fascinated by the golf club. With your coach, really start to understand what you are trying to do with the club head, the clubface and the shaft. If you have a coach who only gets you to focus on what your body is doing and little else, then it may well be time for a change of direction.

As you become more advanced at the game, then it would also be my suggestion to do a lot of work on shaping the ball. Work on hitting the "Nine Shot Shapes". Going from Draw to Straight to Fade with either a High, Neutral or Low flight gives you the variety of trajectories which can lead to greater control of the ball.

When we actually consider the true purpose of the golf swing, we are left with the realisation that it is to control the spin on the ball. Every shot you ever hit will either have the ball spinning where you want it to be or have too much spin that causes the ball to curve away from your target.

By working on the Nine Shots, you also tend to keep your swing in balance. A swing that is producing too much shape on the ball is not in balance. I often think of the words of the legendary Sam Snead when someone asked him how he cured a hook. He said he simply went to the range and "hit slices for a while". The utter simplicity of this yesteryear statement would now be backed up by the most up-to-date neuroscience and psychology; when Snead was focusing on hitting slices to cure the hook, he would by definition have had an external focus of attention. The science may be new but the concepts have been around for a long time.

WHAT IF EXTERNAL FOCUS DOESN'T HELP?

One of the worst aspects of the golf industry I have observed over the years is the "This Is The Secret" mentality. It's based on the concept of a unifying theory of everything concerned with golf and that one theory will fit everyone and every different body and mind. This is plainly ridiculous and it would, therefore, be wrong to say that external focus is the answer that will instantly transform every-one who plays the game of golf.

The science strongly suggests many people will benefit from fo-cusing on external factors as opposed to body parts; but it doesn't mean internal focus is wrong for everybody, or that you cannot make progress by focusing on what your body is doing in the swing. I have worked with a number of great players who I would say have a primarily internal focus. What I have found though, there is a way of using internal focus which is more efficient and tends to allow you to work on your swing in a more brain-compatible way.

Think back to the amazing things we have learned to do over the years – things like walking and talking, which are a fantastic testimony to the capability of the human brain to learn. Now look at how we achieved those feats. If we take the skill of walking, we obviously used a lot of trial and error, we had a lot of guidance, we fell over a lot, but one of the obvious fundamentals to walking was that we learnt to do it *slowly* at first. We took our first tentative steps in a way that gave our brain the time to process and, to some extent, "code" the movement. This fundamental skill obviously had a genetic survival need attached to it. If we didn't learn to walk, we couldn't avoid predators and we couldn't hunt for ourselves. Evolution takes no prisoners and when you see a species survive as we have; it is partly down to efficient learning in adaption to the surrounding environment.

So, evolution apart, what does that have to do with you and your golf game? There is an absolutely fascinating video on YouTube of Ben Hogan talking about how he practised his golf swing. In the film he is stood at the edge of the ocean hitting balls out into the blue yonder; and he describes verbally and physically how he makes lots of *slow motion swings* to ingrain the key moves he wanted in his action. He demonstrates a swing in super slow motion but he actually hits the ball. He doesn't do this as a split drill or a pump and go, he makes the full and complete movement in slow motion. For me, this is the critical key. He is not splitting the swing up into segments, he is not standing there with a beach ball between his legs; he is making a very complete neural map of his golf swing… at a speed that evolution suggests would be the most efficient way of integrating the motion into his game.

When we look at this concept, it would be wonderful for me to say I have discovered a radical and revolutionary way of learning to swing the club better; but, of course, this concept of learning in slow motion has been around for a long time. In the ancient martial art of Tai Chi when you see people stood in groups making lovely swirling, circular motions, they are actually learning fighting techniques. But, they are working at a speed that centuries of wisdom tell us allows the brain to learn better.

There is no doubt in my mind this approach can be a major influence in your developing as a golfer. This is not just my opinion; science is backing this up.

Here is a great piece of information from a tremendous website: **www.bettermovement.org**

Another reason to move slowly and gently is to allow yourself time to approach movement in an exploratory and curious manner, and to put a great deal of attention on the subtle details of the movement.

Becoming more coordinated is essentially a matter of rewiring the neural circuits that control movement. This is an example of a process called Neuroplasticity. Neuroplasticity simply means the brain's ability to change. According to Michael Merzenich and other prominent neuroscientists, attention and awareness are crucial preconditions for neuroplasticity to occur. In other words, your brain is much more likely to get better at a certain activity if you are paying close attention while doing it. Slow movement can help your ability to pay attention to exactly what you are doing when you are doing it.

USE GEARS TO BOOST INTERNAL FOCUS

If you still feel an internal focus would work best for you and you want to improve a certain part of your body motion, then make slow-motion complete and full swings as part of every practice session. Work the "Three Gears".

○ Make your first swing super slow – first gear. Hit three balls in first.
○ The next set should be hit in second gear, which will be around 50% of your normal effort levels. Hit three balls in second.
○ The final set should be close to your normal swing speed. This is third gear. Hit three balls in third.

Do this drill for no more than 30 minutes.

Hopefully, during this chapter, I have given you an opportunity to consider and reassess how you go about working on your golf swing. I never want to be accused of being a "golf is all in the mind" coach when plainly, to have good mechanics and have control over your ball flight is a *huge* advantage. But, you do need to know the best ways to engage your brain in the process of swinging the club better. It isn't just about gaining some information of how to swing the club; you need to know how to integrate that knowledge for it to become an actual physical motion.

Consider what we have discussed. Work with your coach on applying these principles and I am certain your game will benefit. That said, bear in mind no amount of correct practice will ever stop you hitting poor shots.

I have found this concept to be a wonderful
aid to improving your golf swing mechanics.
Go to this link on YouTube:
http://www.youtube.com/watch?v=y6ARlgEuZdk
to see Graeme McDowell working on
this with his short game.

As well as controlling the ball, we have to work equally as hard in controlling ourselves. Let us move on to the next chapter to see just how we can go about doing that.

CHAPTER 2

FREE YOURSELF TO PLAY YOUR BEST GOLF

once sat in on a business seminar with a very successful golf professional who, for years, had run a large business operation. It involved a great number of staff in key positions all related to the game of golf. As he took us through some of the finer details of his business, he suddenly revealed the key to his success over the years, was the quality of his staff. The people in his business, he felt, were the determining factor between success and failure.

A delegate asked the presenter how on earth he had managed to hire and retain so many good people. His initial response set us all back somewhat when he said the first thing he did was to pay very little attention to CVs. "Everybody looks and sounds pretty good on a CV," he said. "If you can't look good on your CV then you really do have problems. But, a CV can never convey the personality and genuine attitude of the individual."

He then went on to describe how the *real* interview started when he informed the candidate they had been short-listed and invited them for a game of golf to discuss the post in question. "This is when the real discovery takes place because the first thing I tell them is the game of golf will be at 6am," he explained. "I listen for their response. If the response is one of enthusiasm, then I *know* I have someone who will be a good timekeeper. If the response is a silent pause, then I know time-keeping will be a big issue!"

The big event though would be the actual game itself. He went on to say how nine holes would reveal to him all he needed to know about the individual concerned. "The game," he argued, "just gives you a window to their soul. You can see how they respond to set-backs, you can see how personable they are as you walk in between shots. You get a sense of how mature they are… but above all else, you can see how good they are at controlling their emotions."

It is many years since I sat in on that seminar, but I have never forgotten it. For me, it was a graphic learning experience of what golf can reveal about us as people. It began to highlight to me how the game of golf *will* find us out. It will reveal our personality, it will test us. But, even more profoundly, *your response to that test will determine how good you get to be at this game.* We will unearth why in the coming pages.

Despite its importance, most of the time, golfers are blissfully unaware of how they act out on the course. Often, I am quite cruel with a player when I start working on his game. I will follow him around the course in a tournament with a camera, but I don't use the camera to show him making any swings or missing putts. The only thing I will have videoed out on the course is what he is doing in between shots. The footage reveals his reactions to what the golf ball has done, his body language and his demeanour. I have lost count of the number of times I have shown these films to players, only for them to shake their head and say: "Well, I am not normally as bad as that!"

It stands repeating: we are all blissfully unaware of how we carry ourselves on the course and how we react to what the golf ball does.

Yet, if we look at the game of golf in terms of duration, your average tournament round will take the best part of five hours… and the time that we are actually playing the game is minimal. About 90% of the game of golf is *not* golf; it is something else.

Do you think that 90% may have some impact on the 10%? And yet, how much time do we actually spend on understanding and working with that 90%? It is the great hidden factor of the game.

As a quick aside, this is another problem with the way we typically practise. Golf is an interval sport – there is a relatively long time between shots. In practice, there is hardly any interval – so we don't get to practise our reaction control. After all, there is always another ball waiting to be hit and to make us feel good.

Yet, the really good news about this part of the game is that unlike the swing, we can become very consistent at controlling ourselves out on the course. We can excel at what we do in the 90% – and when we do, we get much closer to discovering the golfer that we can truly be.

We will go into the details of how you can get better at controlling yourself as we explain the concept of The Three Phases of Golf. But, for now, I think you will find it useful for us to delve a little deeper into why the game of golf is so very revealing of us, and our personalities. The answers explain why so many of us are routinely playing the game under a great weight of pressure that is both unhelpful and unnecessary.

It is incredible to think how a game involving placing a small white ball into a hole in a big field can make us behave in such a strange way. Go to any tournament at any level and watch players closely, and you will see examples of real and genuine fear. You will see people who are literally shaking on the first tee; you will see people who get so incredibly angry, they either outwardly explode or they go into a dark silent world of sulking. You see incredible levels of frustration because the ball has not behaved as they would have liked it to.

People start out on a round of golf chatting happily away to each other. But, as the round progresses, if we could tune into their internal world, we would inevitably hear an incredible level of self-loathing and hatred. And this is what we do for a hobby!

Alternatively you can witness examples of boast and bravado. Perhaps the hacker arriving on the first tee with the big tour bag, the latest must-have equipment, the fancy trousers, designer belt and gel in the hair! Or, maybe you will meet the player heading out to play a game based on achieving the lowest score possible, but whose one real concern is how far he can lace his tee shots with his new super-charged titanium whopper driver! It really is a game that reveals so much about us as individuals.

So what is *really* going on under the surface here? And what game are these folks really playing?

CORE-SELF AND PERFORMER-SELF

To answer this question, I believe we must assess what I consider to be a critical factor in the development of your game. It is a bit deeper than the obvious issues you may have looked at before, such as your grip and backswing, but it illuminates much of what we are looking at in this chapter.

Much of what I have seen on a golf course and experienced my-self in terms of destructive behaviour, comes from one central issue: that at the heart of things we, as human beings, often perceive our-selves as simply not being good enough. We are not valuable enough as people, we tell ourselves, so we have to perform in a certain arena to affirm our self-worth and value.

The problem with this has been summed up wonderfully by the words I read many years ago from Tim Gallwey, who wrote *The Inner Game of Golf.* "If golf has the capability to make you a some-body," he said, "it also has the capability to make you a nobody."

Legendary Social Psychologist, Mihaly Csikszentmihalyi, puts it differently: "The problem is that the more the ego becomes identi-fied with symbols outside the self, the more vulnerable it becomes."

If this is striking some dissonant chords with you, do not be alarmed. In many ways, we all suffer from this to a greater or lesser degree. I am not sure anyone is totally immune. Just be aware that, in effect, what happens to us is we lose sight of the distinction between something we *do* and something we *are.*

the mind factor

As human beings, we all have the same value which is given to us when we are born. Nobody is better or worse than anyone else. We all have a unique, intrinsic value that is essentially our *core-self*, or our *real-self*. The value is simply in being uniquely human. If I am sat in a room with Jack Nicklaus, he would unquestionably be a better golfer than me; but it doesn't make him a better *person* than me. I may be sat in a room with Sir Richard Branson: he is, undoubtedly, a better businessman than me, but all of his wealth does not make him a better person than me.

So, we have our core-self (the things we are) and our performer-self (The things we do). The problem is when we identify too much with our performer-self, we do, indeed, become *very* vulnerable. For example, if I decide my value as a human being is dependent on how many times I strike that little white ball and whether it bounces left or right, then I am constantly going to feel anxious; and, if the results don't match up to some of my expectations, then I will probably get very angry, frustrated and upset… and beat myself up.

This is the fault of nobody; I am not trying to lay blame here. But, it's a pattern I have seen over and over again with young children. They begin to play the game of golf and, initially, it is just about the sheer joy of whacking the ball from A to B. Take a swipe at it, miss it and laugh or take a swipe at the ball, hit it great and laugh. The game creates great joy. Then the parents get involved. Young Freddy shows some ability. He gets to play in competitions. He does well in competitions, he gets some lessons and others hear about how good he is. When young Freddy comes home after playing a competition, if he has done well, he can clearly see he is a worthy child. His parents heap praise on him and, partly bask in the self-reflected glory. Bad score, however, and the response is not quite the same. If Freddy is lucky, he will not be overtly criticised (if he is unlucky, like a lot of kids, he *will* be criticised) but he *will* sense a difference in the response – and he doesn't feel quite so loved any more.

the mind factor

So, to his young subconscious mind, the message is transmitted that good golf = good person and bad golf = bad person, and the die is cast. He will then not be playing golf anymore; he will be playing "What Will They Think Of Me?".

I have just used golf here as an example but this process can and does take all forms, be that academic success or sporting prowess or business endeavours. The message "I am valuable *if* I perform in a certain way" is a very pernicious and destructive virus that can infiltrate our mind and have a lasting effect throughout the rest of our lives.

The ground-breaking work of Carol Dweck, a Professor of Psychology at Stanford University, has highlighted how we should try to praise our kids for their effort and not so much the result of their effort. Dweck has talked about how children tend to become vulnerable when praised for their results as opposed to becoming resilient when praised for their effort.

The big problem for the developing golf mind is that when we gain strokes or affection based on our ability on the course, as opposed to our effort levels, we pile pressure on ourselves and cease actually to *play* the game.

I, for one, can vividly remember playing the game as a youngster and being fearless in the sense the game was about playing shots and taking chances, and the sheer joy of playing good shots. But, as I became relatively successful as a junior, I could sense the people around me beginning to expect results. The feelings of nervousness and anxiety began to increase as my sense of self became more entwined around the outcome of a round of golf. I didn't know this at the time but looking back, I fell out of love with the game because it ceased to be a game. It became an activity to define my own self-worth.

Not for one minute am I saying children shouldn't play in competitions or we shouldn't try to win tournaments with a passion.

What I am saying is, if you can go out on the golf course and have a bad day and realise it is you, the golfer, having a bad day and not you, the person, then you can set yourself free again to *play* golf – or any other sport, for that matter.

The paradox of this is when we are absorbed in play... when we are really fascinated by the task at hand... when we can't wait to get back on the course to work on our game again... then we will play the type of golf we know we are capable of. Because when our core-self is secure in the knowledge our whole identity isn't on the line, the pressure which has been restricting your game is mercifully released.

WHY DO YOU PLAY GOLF?

One of the big influences on my coaching over the years has been Californian Fred Shoemaker, author of *Extraordinary Golf*. I always remember him saying one of the most important questions we can ever ask ourselves is simply "Why do you play golf?" He said the key thing with the question is *never* to take the first answer people give because it is always the answer they think they should give. Things like "I love the challenge" or "I like being outdoors" sound great, but often they are just the answers we have been conditioned to give.

I think this is still a very valid question to ask; the answer will help you understand to what extent you are basing your self-worth on your performance, and how much pressure you are piling on yourself. But, I have developed a few other questions over the years you may find worth asking in an attempt to perhaps explain some of the things you do on a golf course that you don't particularly like about yourself.

Give yourself some time to sit down and really pay attention to the questions and the answers they provoke. Write out your answers in some detail.

- Why do I play golf?
- What other reasons make me want to play?
- Do I sometimes play the game for others?
- Do I love the game or what the game might bring me?
- What game of golf would I like to play?
- What game of golf would allow me to express my true ability?

Answering these questions won't automatically set you free from a lifetime of conditioning, but they will make you more aware. You may become aware there are other strings pulling at your game other than your golf swing. Perhaps, too, you will gain an awareness that, above all else, you have a *choice* of the kind of game of golf you wish to play.

"What am I committed to *today*?" is another very powerful and important question to ask yourself before you play the round of golf. Will it be a game of golf held back by your past conditioning... or will it be a game of golf allowing you to play a game that can give you great joy and happiness?

That joy and happiness may involve you winning multiple major championships or it may just involve you breaking par or even breaking a 100 for the first time. Either way, it will be *your* game, and you will be playing it for your reasons and not the hidden agenda of some long ago-misinterpreted conditioning that has put you and your game under the kind of pressure which is very hard to play with. Set yourself free to *play* golf.

the mind factor

CHAPTER 3

THE THREE PHASES OF GOLF

I can clearly recall a conversation I had with Graeme McDowell after he won the Scottish Open at Loch Lomond back in 2008. He talked to me about how his mind had played tricks on him in the final round. Walking to the 15th tee, he had a cushion of a couple of shots between himself and the chasing pack. He then went on to describe how he was suddenly hit with a random thought he was going to "top" the ball off the 15th tee.

Can you imagine one of the world's best golfers, playing some of the best golf of his career... and suddenly he is convinced he's about to hit a shot that should be the province of a struggling high-handicapper!

As he talked about this, he then stood up to say that this was the moment he finally *fully* realised the importance of all the work we had done over the years on his routines. He made a kind of swaying motion from side to side, and then told me his routine was like a rope he could hang onto during those stormy moments when his mind started to throw him some mental hand grenades.

What this reinforced for me personally was that even the very best players have a mind that *will* play tricks on them. Critical to overcoming these moments is the understanding and application of an *effective routine*.

Since those early days, I have developed a concept of the routine that has been widely accepted and applied by a number of the world's best players. It – and the philosophy behind it – is at the heart of this book.

It is the concept that on *any* golf shot, there are three distinct Phases:

1. The Pre-Shot
2. The Shot
3. The Post-Shot

To get the best out of yourself, you must first be aware of these phases before creating a plan to personalise each step.

Most golfers will only ever look at one of the Phases – the Shot Phase. Some will be aware of the Pre-Shot Phase but very few put the whole package together, which is a shame – for this is how to build a bulletproof system to enable you to get as close as possible to controlling your mind on each and every shot.

At the beginning of the book we talked about the vital component of controlling your attention. When you have understood and applied the Three Phases of Golf, you will be a significant step nearer creating an *attentional focus* that is effective out on the golf course, as opposed to something that just works on the range.

Now let us take each Phase in turn, to understand its role in creating a state of mind that promotes your very best golf.

1 THE PRE-SHOT PHASE

What I am not going to do in this book is to go through any ideas about course management or course strategy. These are areas I would hope you would work on with your PGA professional. I am also going to assume that on each and every shot, you take the time to gather what I would call "essential information". Things like the lie of the ball, the wind and the yardage. Once you have done that, the real work of the pre-swing shot begins.

the mind factor

Let me start by asking you to consider the other sports you play or have played. Whether it's football or basketball, snooker or darts, the object of the game is essentially to send an object to a target. Dart to board, basketball to hoop, football to goal. Most sports pretty much involve that basic formula.

As you think about those other sports, consider where you were looking and what your attention was on when you propelled your object to your target. Treble 20 for the darts player? Pocket for the snooker player? In pretty much every sport you can think of, you will be "looking where you are going" when you send the object to that target. Apart from *one* sport!

In any target-based sport, having a very clear image of where we are going is crucial. Golf is no exception – and yet it is a very unusual sport in the sense we are not actually looking where we are going.

If I stand about 10 feet from you and throw a ball to you – and you catch it and throw it back to me – you will do a pretty good job of hitting the target, i.e. my hand. If I throw the ball to you and ask you immediately to throw the ball back to me but this time with your eyes closed, then you will *still* do a pretty good job.

But what if I were to ask you to catch the ball, close your eyes, keep hold of the ball and count to 10... during which I move to a different location? Do you think you would be anywhere near as effective? Of course not, because your brain has no idea where the target is. Initially, with your eyes closed, you can still hit the target because your brain has retained an image of the target and it can go to work on that image: it still has a very clear task to set to work on. But unfortunately, many golfers are in effect hitting towards a moving target with their eyes closed because they have no concrete way of making sure their brain has retained an *image* of the target or the task at hand.

A critical part of the Pre-Shot Phase is to make sure you have a very clear image of what the target or the task is, in this specific moment in time. The brain is a unique problem-solving machine but you need to give the brain a clear problem for it to solve to be able to go to work. So often, we get so caught up in "golf swing" that we forget "golf game" where we move a ball to a target.

So if we need a very clear image of the target or the task at hand, then surely we need to know what the best way is for our brain to create a workable image it can act upon.

If I said to you now "What is the first thing you will see when you open your front door tonight?" or "What does your best friend look like?" I would guess most of you have just had images of hall clocks or coat stands, or the face of someone you really like. Your brain will have been flooded with a *clear image*. Yet, the critical key here for you to understand is the mechanism inside your head that created that image in your mind. What was it that made the image appear?

The *question* created the image. What does your best friend look like? The question is asked and your brain goes to work on creating the image that supplies the answer. It is wonderfully simple when you consider it. So if questions create clear images, surely the job of *every* golfer on *every* shot is to ask a *quality question* relative to the task at hand. Questions are the answer!

Over the years, I have had many golfers tell me they can't visualise. Their problem is that *trying* to visualise is a bit like trying to sleep; it should just happen but it doesn't. The more we try to see a sharp picture, then the more blurred it becomes.

So when I tell players they don't have to worry about visualising or making images on a shot – they simply need to ask a *quality* question and their brain will go to work – their relief is palpable. To try to visualise or create images is tough, but to ask a quality question is very simple.

Remember what I said earlier: the quality of your life will be determined by the quality of your questions. Can you now see the

the mind factor

gravity of such a statement? The wonderful aspect of questions is they *focus your attention*. If you control your questions, then you will control your attention and, if you control your attention, you *will* be successful in almost any activity.

So what would be an example of a quality question on a given golf shot? This is something that, ultimately, I would like you to personalise; but my all-time three favourites that have proven to be very successful, are:

- What does a good shot look like here?
- What is the shot here?
- What is the target here?

They may look deceptively simple but they can be profound. As we have already stated though, the simplicity lies in asking that quality question on each and every shot you play. Questions become an anchor point in your routine.

By asking this question, you are in effect controlling your mind. You are not trying to be "positive", whatever that means; you are simply creating a mechanism to control your attention and your focus. You are not saying you will hit a good shot; you are providing the *environment* for your brain/body system to work in harmony to give you your best chance of producing the best shot you are capable of in this moment.

What task would you sooner be given? To try to visualise the perfect golf shot? Or simply to ask yourself a quality question on every shot?

TURNING QUESTIONS INTO ANSWERS

When you ask the question, your brain will go to work on finding the answer. You can try it right now, sat here reading this book. Think about the first hole on your golf course. Notice what you see to the left. Notice what you see to the right. Then, simply ask yourself: "What does a good shot look like here?" You will find as you do that, an image of a shot will appear in your mind's eye. It may be a picture of a shot shape, you may answer it verbally or you may get a sense of a feeling of the shot.

Either way, you have now created a very clear *intention* of what you want to do with this shot. Intention is very powerful, and we will return to the concept later.

But for now, having created a very clear intention, you have an opportunity to *feel* the shot you are about to play. You can now take the wonderfully unique chance that golf gives you to "pre-programme" the shot you want to hit. This is the time to *sense* the swing that will produce the shot on which you have set your intention. This is *sensing* the swing as opposed to thinking about swing positions. I hate seeing golfers making "drill swings" or rehearsing a body motion or club motion. This is *not* the time for mechanics; it is the time for feel. Leave mechanics for your skill acquisition sessions on the range.

Instead, my suggestion would be to make a full dress rehearsal of the move you intend to put on the ball. You have established the answer to the question "What does a good shot look like here?" Now you are moving on to its follow-up – "What does this shot *feel* like?" Your dress rehearsal swing will represent the answer to this question. Simulate the swing in its entirety and at the speed needed to produce the shot you have intended.

Programme in to the onboard computer between your ears what you want your body to do. This process of what goes through our mind before you step into the ball is, for me, the area that more coaches should be looking at, as it is where a lot of bad shots are created.

CALM THE SYSTEM

The third and final part of the Pre-Shot Phase is designed to allow your body to take over when you play the shot. For this, you

the mind factor

must deal with one of the greatest obstacles to letting your natural ability shine through. This silent killer of your game is tension.

Tension inhibits the neuromuscular system. It is one of the main reasons your best golf swing resides on the range and you seem to turn into a different player on the golf course. Many years ago, I heard a Tai Chi Master say: "Tense muscles are *weak* muscles and they *forget.*" I didn't realise at the time just how profound those words in fact were. The Tai Chi Master was alluding to the fact tension will not only cost you distance, but it will also create a scenario where it is as though your muscles forget the motion you have practised. In effect, you are now in a different "state" than the one when you learnt the movement. "State-dependent learning" suggests that to perform a task you have practised, you have to be in a similar state when performing as you were when you learnt the move.

The simplest and most efficient way of controlling your tension is to become aware of your breathing. Centuries-old wisdom would suggest it is very difficult to hold on to tension and breathe correctly. Tension and shallow breathing go hand-in-hand... as do relaxation and *deep* breathing. So the final part of your pre-swing is to focus on a *full exhale* before you step into the ball.

Breathe out fully and completely so you feel your stomach retracting back towards your spine. Then you will find yourself taking a full reflex breath in, as you fill your lungs and diaphragm. It is this breath that will activate what's called your parasympathetic nervous system into a relaxation response. You are in effect releasing any tension and creating an optimum state for your body to perform. Every psychology book will tell you that you need to be in the present moment: but if you place your attention on your breathing, you *are* in the moment as opposed to simply trying to be.

The other trigger I would like you to set up in your mind is the belief that once you consciously breathe in as the final part of your pre-shot routine, then you have in effect programmed the computer.

The thinking, planning and preparation are now done. You have in effect done all you can to give yourself the best possible chance in this moment to hit a good shot. It does not guarantee you will hit a good shot, but you have done all that you can to influence the outcome.

In essence, what I would like you to consider is that the breath is a *release* – a release not just of tension but also a release of attachment to the outcome. We know for certain that the ball will do one of three things. It will either go to your intended target or it will go to the left or to the right of your intended target. This you really have to accept as the universal truth that you will *never* have total control over what that golf ball does. But as long as you can walk into the ball knowing you have "done your bit", then you can, indeed, release yourself to play the shot at hand.

2 THE SHOT PHASE

Now all you have to do is employ that Pre-Shot Phase, walk into the ball, switch your mind off and just let the body take over, right? Wouldn't it be nice if it happened that way? The problem is that the mind doesn't stop thinking. It doesn't just switch off. You will still have your attention on something. But what? This for me is the million-dollar question. Where should I place my attention when I am over the ball, and then when I pull the trigger and swing the club? These are the critical moments that will essentially make or break all of the good work you have put in with the Pre-Shot Phase.

If you pick up any golf magazine, you will find literally hundreds of ideas and concepts of what you should focus on during the swing itself. The standard piece of advice would be to think of a move in your swing. Turn the hips, fire the right side, keep your spine angle... the list goes on. These are examples of the internal focus mentioned in Chapter One. Essentially, this puts your attention on *what* you are doing.

Then along came a lot of mind gurus who said you shouldn't be thinking about what you are doing, you should have your attention on the target. "Train it and then trust it" became a powerful mantra. A variation on this theme was the concept of "clear keys' – the idea you should place your attention on something totally unrelated to the action or the outcome itself. So you would be over the ball and you would say "Tr-la-la-la" or "One two, buckle my shoe", anything so long as this didn't involve anything to do with the action or the outcome of the shot.

Years ago, a suggestion from *The Inner Game of Golf* was to say to yourself "Back – Hit" in the sequence of the motion of the golf club. Another idea has been to just be aware of the move you are making without trying to change it.

I have to admit to being horribly confused by all this advice over the years. I would hear psychologists say you should never be thinking about the swing when you are over the ball... and then I would have a major winner tell me that was *exactly* what they had been doing under the most intense pressure, and performing fantastically well!

So the question remains: What should I put my attention on while over the ball and during the motion of the swing? And, more importantly, will this focus of attention make me play good golf consistently?

THE ONE POINT

I am not going to claim ownership of the complete answer to this puzzle; yet I think we can find a big clue in another discipline that has been around for centuries.

A key tenet of meditation is trying to quieten the mind by having your attention held in one place – the "One Point", as I believe it is known in the world of martial arts. Your one point may be the rise and fall of your breath; it may be to look at and observe the flame of a candle; it may be a mantra such as "Om". The focus of your attention is up to you to decide, but the underlying principle is the same. You choose to put your attention in one place for the duration of your meditation session.

Now, as any meditator would tell you, what sounds very simple takes a lifetime to master. In fact, you never master it because there will always be good days and bad days with your meditation when your mind wanders. But you stick with your essential discipline. You stay with your principle. You don't come and go. You stick with the underlying principle of taking time from your day and choosing to place your attention in a designated place and in a disciplined way.

For me, this is as close an answer as I can get as to what we should do over the ball. We need to decide to hold our attention in one place. If I think back to the really bad days on a golf course that I have had, it has usually been when my attention has been jumping around during the swing. I'm willing to bet you could tell me a similar story. I would have had a backswing thought that seemed to hold my mind for the beginning of the swing, but it would always leave the space for other thoughts to come in… and my mind would jump around.

As long as we decide what we are going to place our attention on for the duration of the swing, it doesn't really matter what the subject is. What is critical, is we stay with that commitment through the entire journey of the swing – something which, as any golfer knows, is far easier said than done.

For the golfer, the concept of One Point has four basic options:

THE CLUB

If you feel comfortable with placing your attention on the club during the swing, then pick a part of the club – the head, the shaft, the grip or whatever – and place your attention on that part of the club from start to finish in the swing.

the mind factor

If you choose the club head, you in effect "stay with the club head". You are not trying to do something with the club head; you are simply being with the club head and observing what it does. But your mind is *held* in the One Point which leaves the genius of your unconscious mind clear to do the actual work of moving your body and the club through space.

THE BODY

Again, the same principle applies. You choose a body part to focus on – say your right shoulder. You don't try to move the shoulder in any particular way; you just rest and hold your attention in that spot from start to finish. You are aware of the shoulder as opposed to trying to *direct* it.

THE TARGET

Some golfers play great golf by simply having their attention on the target or the flight of the ball all the way through the swing. The target is their own way of holding attention. It is still a One Point!

UNRELATED FOCUS

This is where all the theories of focusing on a non-task-related subject come together. If you hum a tune during the swing, if you say "Tra-la-la" during the swing, you are still embracing the concept of a One Point.

Hopefully, this will give you your one personal menu and agenda with which to work. It is up to you to choose where you put your attention during the actual time you swing the club. You will need to work and experiment to discover which of the four options works the best for you, but you must decide on one and to get the best out of your game, you then need to stay with that focus for the entirety of the swing.

Time and time again when I see players "get" this concept, they set themselves free from the fruitless search for swing tips and secrets. They understand that if the conscious mind is held in a place of interest with the One Point, their own natural genius can begin to emerge. As Tiger Woods once put it, "It is as if my body just takes over."

3 **THE POST-SHOT PHASE**

I firmly believe that the greatest opportunity for you to improve as a golfer this year is to fully understand and apply the principles I am about to share with you on what happens after the shot is hit. It is an area that is virtually *never* considered in any instruction – yet it is the part that may well have the biggest effect on your game.

Take your seat on a Saturday night to watch some golf on the TV and the standard fare you will be subjected to will include the mind-numbing spectacle of the "experts'" view on why a top-class golfer has suddenly hit a ball way to the left or way to the right.

The "expert" will know the ball has gone to the left or right: and then as he "*analyses*" the swing, he then proceeds to tell you a story as to why that shot has been so wild. "Clearly on that one, you can see how Tiger got the club a little too much from the inside, he got "trapped" and he then "flipped" his hands through impact." What absolute genius he must possess to be able to feel *exactly* what the great golfer felt and then be able to pass all of that wisdom down to us mere mortals! This particular scenario has been played out so many times, it makes me want to weep.

Yet, this doesn't even tell half the story. Let's just rewind the play a little bit to what happened *before* the shot went to the left. Let's look back at the last green where we see the great player miss a short putt and storm off the green, slamming his putter into the side of his bag

the m nd factor

en route. He races to the next tee with his head down, berating his poor caddie for giving him such a poor read. He is absolutely *seething* with anger and with that seething anger comes various chemical reactions within his body. The release of stress hormones such as cortisol excite the system, and he is basically in flight-or-fight mode as those chemicals tell his brain there is a serious issue here.

Now, from the point he reacts so badly to the last previous shot to the beginning of the next shot, he has a huge amount of work to do to get his system back into some kind of equilibrium and balance. If he keeps beating himself up and berating himself, do you think the state he arrives at the next shot could possibly have some impact on the shot he is about to play? It amazes me how we never look at this part of the game.

Any single golf shot you will ever hit will, in itself, have absolutely no meaning other than the meaning you assign to it. Let me repeat that because it is of tremendous importance. *No golf shot you ever hit has any meaning to it other than the meaning you assign to it.*

Yet, what is important is not so much the meaning of the shot but your reaction to that shot. It is one of the very few areas of the game that is totally up to you to control. With the best will in the world, you will never totally control the flight of the golf ball as we have discussed, but you *can* control your reaction to the golf ball.

Consider this. If you could play a round of golf in a state of equanimity whereby you accepted whatever the ball did and you then went ahead and executed a perfect routine on the next shot, do you think if you did that over and over again, time after time, round after round, you might just find out how good a golfer you could really be?

Well, probably none of us will ever totally get there. But I promise you if you make a lifelong commitment to dealing with what the golf ball does and understanding the essential chaos the game will throw at you, there is a distinct possibility you will become a very difficult golfer to beat and you will begin to play a game that will very pleasantly surprise you.

Developing the skill of acceptance with a good Post-Shot routine is, I would say, the *ultimate* mental skill all others can be built upon. If you don't build a good Post-Shot routine, it won't matter how good your Pre-Shot routine is because you will not stick to it; your brain will hijack your best efforts to go through your routine and you will then suffer over the ball. However, develop a great Post-Shot routine and you will give yourself a terrific chance of becoming a better player.

HOW TO BUILD A POST-SHOT ROUTINE

The first thing is to admit to yourself it is an area you need to work on (I have never met a golfer for whom this isn't the case!). From here, examine your current Post-Shot habits. I call them habits because I can guarantee you will have a habitual response to the vagaries of your shot outcomes on the course. Take some time to consider some of the poor rounds you played in the past couple of years. Bring some of those rounds to mind and then create a list of your five worst rounds defined by the way that you controlled yourself.

Write that list out. Then write out this heading:

COMMON THEMES

- What are some of the regular ways I react badly to poor shots?
- What am I doing both internally and externally?
- Would other people "know" I was having a bad day?

the mind factor

○ What sort of things are going on inside my head?
○ Do I get aggressive with myself, or do I start to moan and whine?
○ In what tone of voice do I speak to myself?
○ What am I showing on the outside?
○ What is my body language like?
○ How do I respond to other people?
○ Do I just withdraw into my own little shell and decide I don't want to "get in the way"?
○ How have I behaved on a golf course in the past?

Write out a thorough and detailed description of you at your worst!

Please do that *now!*

If you do nothing else from the information in this book, *please* take action on this, as you will be rewarded.

Now, how did that go? As you sit reading your description of yourself and how you handled adversity, how does it make you feel? Given your answers, what do you feel are the chances of you fulfilling your potential of becoming the best player that you can be?

For many players, when I get them to do this exercise, it is the beginning of a major shift in their attitude to the game. As they read the description, they realise how mentally poor they are at the game. They begin to realise just how destructive their lack of emotional control on the course actually is.

The purpose of this exercise is to actually bring to life and raise awareness of something that for most people is totally unconscious. They are blissfully unaware of the baggage they carry around with them on the course.

Once you have done this exercise and brought these issues to life, you can then ask yourself a very simple but important question: "If I continue like this, will I *ever* get the best from my game?"

If your answer is a yes, then well done – you are in the tiny minority of people who control themselves well on the course. You can just pass Go and move on to the next chapter and perfect some other skills.

If you are like the majority though, and you recognise what you have been like, again well done because you have seized upon a tremendous opportunity to improve – here and now.

When I get tour players actually to write this out, it is often strange to observe how embarrassed they are as they reflect on how much the Post-Shot Phase has cost them in their career to date. It is the act of writing it out that is the key though: just to think about it has little or no impact. When these thoughts and reflections become actual written words, the dynamic definitely seems to shift.

When we write out our current story we can then begin to edit our future story. Once you have done this you can then commit to the future you want for your game and yourself.

Simply write out how you are going to be different from now on.

- ○ How will I respond to poor shots?
- ○ How will I be in the face of the inevitable setback?
- ○ What will others notice?
- ○ What will be different about my body language?
- ○ What will I be like after the ball has left the club?

Again, write out a thorough and complete description of how you will be so different in those crucial moments after the ball and club have met each other and it has been sent on its way.

By writing down this description, you are, in effect, "future pacing" your new behaviour in your mind's eye. You are mentally rehearsing a new set of behavioural patterns. You are creating a new story of how you will be.

the mind factor

To complete the exercise, I also want you to write out two more small lists. The first is:

What will happen if I continue with my current patterns?
List the effects on your game and your life.

The second is:

What will be the benefits of my new behaviour and my improved Post-Shot routine?
Again, this is important because you are giving your brain some very powerful reasons to replace one set of patterns with an effective new structure.

Unfortunately, as I am sure you know, ingrained habits are not so easily erased. The work now begins in implementing these strategies. But you can and you will if you follow these three simple rules for the next 10 rounds that you play.

RULE 1: Write it down

Before every round, write out on a card the size of a scorecard what you are committed to in terms of your Post-Shot routine. Describe the you who will be out on the course today. This is so important because you have now made an active commitment to your new pattern. Again, in writing it out *before* you play, you are mentally rehearsing what you are going to do.

RULE 2: Tell others about your commitment

When we let others in on the plan, we are much less likely to fall off track. Having told our friends how much better we will be, we don't want to bear their ridicule if we fail to make good on our confidence.

RULE 3: Score yourself!

Let's say that in Rule 1, you have written down a commitment to maintain good body language in between shots – keeping your posture up and your eyes above the flag. If you play the first hole and you carry out your intention, award yourself a single tick on the scorecard. If you don't and you fall back into old patterns, then you must give yourself an X.

The goal is to obviously score 18 ticks. Just imagine the accomplishment you will feel if you complete 18 holes with 18 ticks. You will know that today, whatever the scorecard says, you have done your absolute best and you have controlled yourself. Think about the intense feeling of pride you will start to feel as your tick scores increase. You are also employing a trick of turning your own natural competitive nature back on itself and playing a game you can actually win!

I guarantee when you start doing this, you will be nowhere near 18 ticks. But as you stick with it and persevere, you will begin to join a very elite club of golfers who can sit in the clubhouse after a game, knowing they have done everything they could do that day.

the mind factor

CHAPTER 4

THE GOLF COURSE

I t may seem strange to you reading a golf instruction improvement book to find a chapter written about the golf course itself. Yet, I have found over the past few years with the advance in technology, science, biomechanics, psychology and the like, the one thing consistently never to get a mention is the golf course! Among all of the wonderful information we have, we seem to have overlooked the actual scene of battle – and its importance.

Most of the scientific testing taking place in golf today is done with a player in a fixed location on a range. Here, he is analysed for anything from the amount of shoulder rotation he makes to the path his putter takes. Yet, in so many ways, this is a fundamentally flawed procedure because it does not take into consideration the true playing environment – the course – and what that actually does to our mind/body system.

One thing social psychology has proven without a shadow of a doubt over the years, is the effect *context* has on us. We literally become different people depending on the context we find ourselves in. You would behave in a very different way and feel a very different set of emotions if you sat on your own in a library as opposed to being with a group of fellow football fans standing on a terrace during an important game.

Many years ago, Philip Zimbardo carried out the Stanford Prison experiment. Students were taken into a "pretend" prison and given the role of either a prison guard or a prisoner. Within a few short days, they started to act out the roles they had been given. Even though the environment was supposedly a pretence, the illusion was powerful enough that the students who had been allocated the role of being prison guards started to behave sadistically towards the "inmates", who were actually their fellow students.

The experiment had to be stopped very quickly because in a very short space of time, the behaviour of the students in the context of prison had become very scarily too realistic and too representative of what perhaps goes on in a real prison situation. Normal, rational and sane students, behaving totally irrationally... just because they had been placed in an environment which triggered certain behaviours.

The environment or the context we find ourselves in *will* trigger certain behaviours, emotions and responses. Understand this fact and you start to realise the importance of the golf course as you seek to improve your game.

Just think for a moment about the unique environment the golf course provides you. You are in a situation where you are with other people you may or may not like; you are faced with a single shot unique in the sense you will *never* be faced with this shot again in your life. The conditions, the lie, the weather conspire to make this a totally singular moment in time and you *have* to adapt to that specific situation.

KNOW YOUR OPPONENT

I often ask young players: "Who is your opponent at golf?" They will usually say "Myself" at first. Wrong. So then they will say "The golf course." Wrong again in my opinion! I firmly believe your real opponent at golf is the course designer. The man or woman who designed this golf course you are standing on, crafted the holes in such a way he or she is trying to get you to do certain things, to fall into certain traps, to take on certain shots.

To consider the course designer your opponent is to set in motion a wonderful change of mind set, whereby you begin to really look at

the mind factor

the golf course for the first time. You start to formulate a plan as to how you can best negotiate that golf course with the shots you have available to you. When you begin to look at the game this way, then you can truly begin to focus your attention on things that are actually worthwhile.

Remember at the beginning of the book when we said your attention was a very simple thing, insofar as it is either on something useful or not useful? This is at the heart of this proposal. Focusing on the golf course and what the course designer is trying to get you to do – and coming up with your own plan – is eminently a useful focus of attention because it is then totally up to you what you do with that plan.

The great thing about golf is that "Nobody can golf your ball"! We can't get tackled, we can't get punched... not even Tiger Woods can come up and move your golf ball. Yet, it never ceases to amaze me how many people play golf focusing on other people who have absolutely no influence on their own game, unless they let them! It always fascinated me to hear people say that this player or that player is playing today. Big deal! They cannot influence what you and your golf ball do unless you transfer your attention and your power over to them.

I found it interesting to discover that in the years when Tiger Woods dominated the game totally and won numerous majors, he almost always won when leading going into the final round. Yet, apparently, Woods" final round stroke average was not outstandingly low. The players who were in contention with him almost inevitably fell away. Their final round stroke averages tended to by quite high. What do you think some of the game's best players were putting their attention on when they played with the great man? The golf course, or playing with Tiger Woods?

I am not saying this is easy and that you can suddenly flick a switch and become oblivious of anything on a golf course other than your own ball and the course. But, I am saying you can at the very least begin to have the intention to think in that way – to have your precious attention in a productive place as opposed to a destructive place.

HOW TO DEVELOP
YOUR ON-COURSE SKILLS

1 TAKE THE "COURSE WALK"

I remember many years ago being at the legendary Fred Shoemaker Golf School in Carmel Valley, California. One of the exercises Fred got us to do out on the golf course, was to do what he called the "Course Walk". He had us play a couple of holes in total silence and to become aware of what we noticed with the experience. Then he had us walk a couple of holes with the task of becoming aware of things we hadn't noticed before.

With the first exercise, I remember being amazed at how uncomfortable it felt to play in a four ball in total silence and how that made me become even more "internal" in my mind. I started to become acutely aware of how much chatter there was going on in the inside of my head: while there was no noise in the four ball, I more than made up for it with what was going on within the space between my ears. It made me acutely aware that when playing in tournaments, the social side of the game was very secondary to my score. I realised how much I withdrew into my self-imposed torture.

The second exercise was the *big* breakthrough though because as soon as I asked myself the question "What have I not seen before?" I began to become extraordinarily aware of the beauty surrounding me. It was helpful we had been given a stunning Southern California day but I really began to notice the incredible richness of the envi-

the mind factor

ronment – the wildlife, the sights and sounds, the contours of the fairways, the cut of the grass and the texture of the sand.

I noticed for the first time in a very long while, the feeling of the gentle breeze cooling my skin and the sense of being alive just by walking down a fairway on a golf course. It made me painfully aware of how little attention I had ever paid to what was actually going on around me, as I usually played the game locked into a list of expectations and aspirations.

We forget golf is a social game played in a wonderful context, and that these elements are not being looked at when we work at our game on the range. I know I am banging a now-familiar drum, but when you have a static position on the range with a perfect lie, the next shot always waiting for you, no time delay between this shot and the next and nobody with you, then there is not the slightest resemblance to the real game.

Try Fred's exercise for yourself. Walk some holes in a four ball in silence and notice what effect that has on you. Play some holes with the question in your mind of "What have I *not* noticed before?"

2 BACK-TO-FRONT GOLF

The main exercise I want you to do though is something I recommend to all of the top players I work with. It is also something Jack Nicklaus was famed for doing.

I want you to go out onto the course and start at the 18th green and walk the course *in reverse*. Yes! That is right. I want you to go out without your clubs and walk the course backwards. Just imagine now if you were standing in this moment at the back of your 18th green. What would you really see?

If I, myself, think of the course where I do a lot of my own coaching – the ruggedly beautiful Manchester GC and the 18th hole in particular. I see a large space to the left of the fairway where the approach would be relatively flat and give me a good line into the whole of the green. I see I really don't want to hit the ball too far down the right hand side because the land falls away dramatically. I see there is no real benefit to taking on the hole with a driver. I see clearly the way the green falls and the best area to putt from. As I walk down the fairway and I look back to the green I see what the clever course designer, Harry Colt, is trying to get me to believe. He wants me to believe it is very tight down the left hand side, so I will tend to aim a bit more to the right and be drawn into his trap of a sloping lie and a run-off into heavy rough. As I stand on the tee I can see what he is up to and how he has been clever enough to camouflage what is really going on with the hole.

In short, I can see a way of playing the hole I wouldn't ordinarily see playing it the normal way. By walking from the green backwards, I have a totally different perspective on the way that the hole is set up. In effect, I can see the hole for what it really is as opposed to what the course designer wants me to perceive.

I guarantee if you do this on your home course, the one you have played hundreds of times and the one you think you know, you will be amazed at what you actually begin to see for the first time. By walking the course this way, you can fall in love with the challenge of cracking the puzzle the course designer has set for you. You will start to see how you could play the course with the tools you have available to you. If nothing else, and at the absolute least, you will have a wonderful walk in nature and you will get to see just what a stunning opportunity a golf course can be to interact with the natural world.

I am not going all touchy-feely here: I am just asking you to look at the game through a slightly different lens than the one that has you transfixed by swing positions and scores. I guarantee by doing this, you will see the game differently. When they do this, many golfers

the mind factor

recognise they have been playing the game in something of a daze – a daze of indifference to what is going on that has been engineered by the culture of golf that pays homage only to the score. Of course the score matters – but if you are not producing the scores you think that you are capable of, then it might just be time to change the lens through which you look at the game.

3 CONTROL EXPECTATION: MANAGE THE PEOPLE YOU PLAY WITH

We would all like to think we are masters of our own destinies, that we control the rudders of our own ships. I used to think this until I began to realise the *unconscious* effect other people were having on me, and the powerful influence this had.

Make no mistake, the people you spend a significant time with *will* influence your golf game and, on a wider scale, your life as a whole. Do you play golf with the same people over and over again? Do you play with golfers who are better than you? Do you keep playing at the same time each week? All of these factors could make a massive contribution to why your game and the improvement you crave is not forthcoming.

Consider this stunning piece of research by Dr Rose McDermott of Browns University, Rhode Island. In a study conducted with more than 12,000 Americans over a 60-year period, she discovered that if a close friend of yours got divorced then *your* chances of getting divorced went up by an astonishing 75%! Even if a friend of a friend got divorced, then your chances of suffering the same fate went up by 33%.

As I said, we are unconsciously affected by the actions and also the expectations of others in a profound way. With the now famous

Pygmalion Effect – the more expectation is placed on someone, the better they perform – it has been proven the law of expectancy can be very strong.

In a well-known study of the Israeli Army by Don Eden at the Tel Aviv University, Eden found a sample of 100 soldiers with at least 11 years" service. These men were selected to attend a combat command course that was run by four experienced training officers. The instructors were given an allocation of 25 trainees. Four days prior to the start of the training, the instructors were given a brief about their students. They were told all the soldiers had been thoroughly tested and given ratings of CP (Command Potential). They were told that based on the CP scores, each trainee had been designated as having High CP (High Command Potential), Regular CP (Regular Command Potential) or UCP (Unknown Command Potential). Each instructor was given individual details of each soldier and their specific CP rating. The four groups had equal numbers of the three categories. During the training, the instructors were asked to rate their soldiers" CP on a scale during the training process.

Those soldiers who had been given a High CP were rated about 15 points higher on a conventional 100-point scale.

The instructors did not know that the soldiers had been randomly assigned and had never actually been given a CP score! The expectation of the instructors had influenced their judgement: but it has also been proven the expectation of others can and does influence our own individual performance.

Just imagine the potential ramifications of this. When you play in your regular four ball, could the expectations of the other three actually have some bearing on the outcome? You bet it does! Based on the social psychology research, it is clear that if the others in your four ball expect you to putt poorly, then you will tend to fulfil that role. On the other hand, if they have a positive expectation, then that will subliminally influence you, too. To a greater

the mind factor

extent than you might imagine, you play like a 10-handicapper because the buddies you always play with expect you to play like a 10-handicapper.

A tough as this may be to take on board, if you are not happy with your progress at the game, then you really need to take a look at who you play the most golf with. I am not saying you abandon your friends because that is such an important part of the game. But I am saying take the opportunity to play with other players. Seek out better players. Change the context of the game you play.

I have seen this work on so many levels over the years. I remember when I played as a junior, there was one club in Leeds called Sand Moor that just kept on producing great junior golfers. Why? Well, do you think that if your friend, who you play with regularly, sees their own game dramatically improve, it may affect your thinking?

I don't think it is any coincidence that when Graeme McDowell won the US Open in 2010, his great buddy Rory McIlroy followed him the very next year to the same major win; or that the other golfer who had been part of the scene at Portrush, Darren Clarke, chalked up his own major win at the Open Championship the year after. The brain says: "If *he* can do it, then surely I can too!"

Take a very close look at this because it *is* influencing your game.

4 LEARN HOW TO PRACTISE ON THE COURSE

Most golfers spend an inordinate amount of time on the range but as we have discussed, very little time on the golf course itself.

I think we are massively missing an opportunity to practise on the course. I am not suggesting you fall out with the Greenkeeper by shelling 10 balls off every tee; but with a little thought, taking your practice mode to the course can make a very valuable contribution to your game. Many players I have worked with improved enormously with this single concept.

Here would be my list of recommended course practice that I am sure once you get into, you will find will have a huge bearing on your game:

WORST BALL

Many years ago I heard Sir Nick Faldo say golf is not about how good your good is but how bad your bad is! I couldn't agree with him more. Improving your scoring is really not so much about improving your good shots – they tend to take care of themselves. It is about reducing the negative and destructive effects of your bad shots. With that in mind, I want you to play some regular sets of nine holes with the toughest drill of them all – "Worst Ball"!

Hit two tee shots. Take the worse of your two drives. Hit two approaches from there. If the first hits the middle of the green but the second misses, bad luck – you have to take the miss. Hole the first one from six feet for a par but, unfortunately, it is not a par until the other ball has also been holed.

It is an awfully demanding and frustrating game but it will show you just how bad your bad is. But more than anything, it shows you how much easier the real game seem when you only have to hole one ball to make your pars and birdies.

Please only play Worst Ball for 9 holes – I don't want to be accused of cruelty to golfers!

Another variation of this game is to play with an opponent. You both hit two tee shots. He gets to pick which of the two shots you play next, and you get to pick his.

the mind factor

IRON OFF EVERY TEE

Many players complain about their home course being relatively easy and then, when they go to play tougher championship courses, they get caught out by having to go into so many greens with long irons and hybrid clubs. By playing your home course with only irons off every tee, you can simulate this effect for when you play elsewhere. Instead of going into a tight little green with a wedge, you are suddenly faced with a 6-iron.

This exercise upholds the key principle of making a part of your practice more difficult than the game itself – just as footballers practise with a small ball, or sprinters run with extra weight. But because you are doing this on the course as opposed to just on the range, its value is optimised. Just imagine the confidence you could take from knowing you could get the ball round in a decent number with just irons off the tee. It also gives you the assurance that if you are struggling with direction off the tee, you can drop down to your irons and still score.

WEDGE 9

There is no doubt in my mind that one of the main reasons Luke Donald became World Number One for a period of time was the fact he became absolutely deadly from 100 yards in. I guarantee if you can improve in this area, you will score lower. Obviously, you will need to work on your pitching technique on the range and your trajectory control. But out on the course, during a nine-hole practice, play your normal ball – but on each hole drop a second anywhere from 30 to 100 yards from the pin. See how many you get up and down in two.

Score it on your card to make yourself accountable. If you start to average more than five out of 10 with this game, you are really in business. You are amongst the very best. At first, your score will be significantly worse than this, but stay with it and do it regularly. You will be rewarded for your efforts.

DELIBERATE MISS

This may sound counterintuitive but I want you to go out and play nine holes and miss each green on purpose. Aim at a bunker or aim at a spot to the right, left, short or long… it doesn't matter, as long as your goal with your approach is to make sure you do *not* hit the ball onto the green.

The object of this rather strange exercise is to see how many times you can get up and down from around the green to salvage your score.

The game is great fun as it takes any pressure off trying to hit perfect or even solid shots. But further, just imagine how you might feel if you've deliberately missed each of the nine greens but you have still managed to put a decent score together. What might that do for your confidence in being able to still score when your game is less than 100%?

I have known good players play this game for a while and get to the point that they can still score close to par missing all the greens. They report back on the confidence it gives them, knowing they don't have to be perfect in a tournament round to be able to put a score together. Again, though, it is just another example of thinking differently by doing a good portion of your work *on the course*, and using your creative imagination to get the ball into the hole.

NO PIN

Play a full round of golf and go out with the mind-set there are no flags on the greens. When it comes to playing your approach shot, you simply look at the middle of the green and nothing else. You just aim to play dead centre – even if it is a short hole and you could go for the pin.

When you play this game, you will probably be surprised to find just how many greens you are able to hit in regulation. It will really hit home to you how many of the mistakes we make in our approach play are through being suckered into going for the flag. Remember our initial premise that the real opponent is the course designer and his on-course team – which includes the Greenkeeper, tucking the flags into certain positions.

This game will also help you determine whether you need to become a more conservative type of player to get the best from your game. I would never argue golf should become an ultra-defensive and timid game – sometimes you really *should* be going at the pin – but this game will reveal a way of thinking which could be very useful to your game management, and future development. Find out which approach works best for you.

CHAPTER 5

ON THE GREEN

We have all heard the statistics about how important putting is to your overall score – that it accounts for nearly half of our shots and how there are no real physical limitations to our improvement. I want to say from the outset I *firmly* believe you will hole more putts with a good stroke as opposed to a bad one, but I am not going to deal here with the stroke in isolation. I am going to assume you will do what it takes to work on your stroke from a technical point of view. My mission here is to provide you with a mind set geared much more to success than the one you currently employ – in effect, to get the best out of your current stroke.

I love the old story about the genius coach, Harvey Penick, and what he is supposed to have said to Tom Kite and Ben Crenshaw on the evening before they were about to begin their careers on the PGA Tour. Apparently, Tom Kite asked Mr Penick that if there was one single piece of advice he would give to the both of them which would have the most impact on their forthcoming careers, what would it be? Harvey Penick looked at them both and simply said: "Make sure you go to dinner with good putters."

Twenty years after first hearing the story and not really under-standing the genius behind those few words, I now fully understand what the wise old coach was getting at. If you went to dinner with good putters, what do you suspect the conversation would be like? What do you think good putters tend to talk about? What do you think good putters tend to focus on?

Over the years working in the game, I have never ceased to be amazed how there is still this pernicious undercurrent that there is something wrong in being a good putter. To this day, I still hear phrases like "He can't hit it but he is a real blade merchant" or "He would never be on tour if he couldn't putt". By the same token, how many times have you sat with people who are hopeless putters but who somehow seem to wear that mantle like a badge of honour?

I firmly believe to become a really great putter, you need to fall in love with the *idea* of being great on the greens. You need to talk about holing putts. You need to be proud of the fact you can get the ball around the course when you are playing less than 100%, by virtue of your artistry with the short stick. You need to promise yourself you are going to avoid conversations with people who seemingly want to brag about how hopeless they are on the greens and parade their "great ball striker" title before you. You want to be able to record and recall your successes. You may need to put up with some banter and ribbing about how many putts you hole as you turn the corner and start to enjoy success on the greens. Yet, one thing I do know for certain after years working with this particular area at the highest level is, that *nobody* can hit the ball well enough to compensate for being a bad putter. Even the greatest ball striker of them all, Ben Hogan, was driven to distraction by his inability to execute what should be the simplest of tasks, rolling a ball a few feet into the hole.

So, where does becoming a great putter actually begin? Well, as I have already stated, I do think you need to build some decent mechanics so you have some control over the path and face of the putter, but a good stroke does not mean you will become a good putter. I have seen some wonderful, technically sound putting strokes that have yielded little or no results once the player has taken his stroke out onto the course. I firmly believe becoming a good putter for the long term, requires you to start with what I call a "consistent opinion".

The dictionary definition of opinion is *a personal view, attitude, or appraisal*. I believe you have to have an opinion that supports you when you walk onto the greens. An opinion you can stay with through thick and thin, no matter what your results may be. In effect, an opinion you can rely on in all conditions and all circumstances.

So what opinions are worth looking at in terms of holing putts?

A lot of people say you should have a positive mind set when you walk onto the green, that you should believe you are going to hole this putt. Sounds simple and easy and should be effective. It is the logical first opinion that has been around for as long as the game has been played. But, does being positive really work in the long term, week after week, round after round?

If this attitude or opinion is the one you currently use and you are a great putter, then you should definitely keep with it. Yet, if we look a little deeper, we might see positive thinking isn't all it is cracked up to be. Let's take an imaginary example of Joe who has just read a good book on "being positive" and he decides he is going to go out on the course believing he is going to hole everything.

So he is on the first green and he has a 6ft putt. He tells himself "This is going in." He convinces himself this ball *will* drop into the hole. He fills his mind full of positive statements about what is about to happen.

He then goes through his routine, he lines the putt up, convinced this is going in, he then hits the perfect putt at the perfect pace on the perfect line... Now, does the ball definitely go in?

Not definitely! All of Joe's future predictions about what the ball was *going* to do didn't quite work out, despite the fact he hit a perfect putt. Why? Because, his ball running towards the cup, may have hit a spike mark that threw it offline.

There are a lot of outside factors involved in that little ball finding its way into the cup – and no amount of positive thinking will guarantee it happening. In effect, saying you *will* hole a putt is a future prediction based not so much on an absolute truth but on a *projection*.

Joe's problems then get compounded by the fact he plays a few more holes with this positive mind set and the ball *still* doesn't drop! After a while, it reaches a point where Joe's mind gets so sick of all these positive thoughts that it jumps the fence and says "To hell with this, I can't hole a thing".

He now becomes convinced he can't hole anything and he becomes ultra-negative. He tells himself there is almost no point in even trying to hole the next one because he is bound to miss.

He looks at the next putt, convinced he is going to miss, sends the ball somewhere on line with a half-hearted stroke. Now, does the ball definitely miss because of that negative attitude and projection? Of course not, because positive or negative projections are simply a forecast of what may or may not happen. They are a prediction of a perceived outcome that is not 100% under our control.

The real problem with positive or negative thinking is that the mind gets very busy and agitated over a projected future. In many ways, positive thinking can, of course, be better than negative thinking. But, in all of my time involved in the game, all it does for the vast majority of golfers is create an agitated mind that isn't really focused on what it needs to be focused on the task at hand, but on what may or may not take place in the future.

When I have talked to great putters, they very rarely tell me they try to be positive; but they do tell me their mind is very still and very calm. Positive thinking is, in effect, just more and more thinking when, in fact, we should be thinking less.

If positive thinking isn't the way forward and we obviously don't want to be negative, then what sort of opinion should we take with us onto the greens? What opinion could we hold dear to us that would keep our mind calm and set us free to hole more putts?

NEUTRAL THINKING

I firmly believe the way out of all of this insanity is to embrace what I call "Neutral Thinking". Neutral thinking is a tool that keeps

the mind factor

you grounded, closer to the present moment. It is a tool to keep your mind much quieter than the crazy busyness of artificial and forced positivity. Neutral thinking may seem to be the slightest of semantic shifts but I am convinced when you work with it and see it in action, you will be more than pleasantly surprised.

How do we do that?

You are about to learn a *critical* word you can begin to employ on the greens that will see your mind sail from choppy seas to tranquil waters.

So let's get back with Joe again.

On the 13th green, he is faced with another 6ft putt. He hasn't holed much at all today. But as he begins his process, he simply asks himself the question: "Is it *possible* I could hole this putt?"

Now, as you attempt to answer that question for Joe yourself, what is the outcome? Despite everything that may or may not have happened so far in the round, is it possible Joe can hole this putt here and now, in this moment? And the answer is of course yes, it *is* possible. We are not saying it will go in, nor are we saying it won't. What we are saying is that right here and now it is *possible* to hole this putt.

Can you see the simple but vitally important shift? There are no predictions, there is nothing to get in our way other than the openness of this task in this moment and a mind set saying it is possible.

Is it possible to drive a ball 500 yards into the wind? No. Is it possible to have a hole-in-one on a par five? Unfortunately, no. But, it is possible to walk on a green and look at a putt and have an open and calm mind, grounded in the here and now, which is able to focus on the appropriate details of the task ahead. Then the brain needs to let the body take over and work its magic.

The beauty of neutral is it is pragmatically optimistic as opposed to being fantasy-based positive or downbeat negative. The opinion of neutral actually sets you free to just *be* and then to *do*. I believe one of the bravest things a golfer can do on the course is to stay open to "possible". I am absolutely certain if you can train yourself to be in neutral by the use of the word "possible", then you are well on your way to becoming a very tough opponent to beat.

For me, in an ideal world, you would begin using "possible" right from the first green. The only time you run out of "possible" is on the last green – as long as you decide to commit to that open mind which created the space necessary to focus appropriately on the right things. The game will undoubtedly challenge you to move away from "possible'; but by having the discipline and the strength of your convictions, you can stay brave enough and determined enough to start – and end – with that mind set. It is a wonderfully simple but potentially powerful shift in attitude.

INTENTION

The great value of "possible" as a mind set is that it allows you to focus your intention. Once you have accepted it is possible for this ball to go into the hole, what do you *intend* to do?

There is a subtle but important difference between an intention and a projection. When we say we are going to hole this putt, that is a projection into an unknown future, and you bring in all of the thought gremlins we have already discussed. A projection is future-based.

But, if your *intention* is to roll this ball on a line an inch outside the right lip, then you are grounding yourself in the task that is before you. You aren't falling into the trap of saying you will hole the putt only to court disappointment. But you *are* saying you intend the ball to travel on the line you have picked. You are again still in neutral – not positive or negative – but you are absorbed in the task as opposed to the outcome of the task.

the mind factor

Nick Faldo once said he felt a clear intention was one of the most powerful of forces on a golf course. The beauty of it is that when it is very clear, your intention will focus your *attention*. Yes, our old friend attention comes back into the mix. But now on the greens, we have the makings of a formula or system for holding your attention.

PUTTING ATTENTION

Once you have stated your intention, on what should you place your precious attention?

Time on the putting surface is somewhat different from the rest of the game. It is, in effect, a confined space where you and your playing partners go about your business in a pretty orderly fashion and in a reasonably short space of time. That time and how you use it is critical.

- ○ You walk on the green open to the idea that holing putt facing you is possible and you can hole it.
- ○ You intend to go through your routine and set the ball off on a certain line that will give you the best possible chance of success.

But how do you get to that point where you are very clear on what the putt is going to do?

My view, first of all, is that when reading a putt less is more. We tend to putt well as youngsters and then as we get older, we tend to get worse. Why is that? For me, the main reason is that the older we get, the more we think and analyse; and the more we do that, we more we get in the way of our wonderful subconscious system which has incredible powers as long as we don"t stall it with excess information.

If you look at a putt from behind the hole, you are gaining information from in my opinion the most important source – the line on which the ball needs to travel to enter the hole. Some, who would dispute this, prefer to look from behind the ball. They look from the other side and they also look from either side. Again, if you do this and you are a great putter then please carry on. But, if you are struggling with your putting and you do take a lot of "looks", then I would ask this question: once you have read the putt from behind the ball, does further analysis make you more or less certain of the line?

For many golfers, the more they look at the line from different positions, the more they see. Rather like the man with four watches who never knows the right time. The more they see, the more unsure they become. I would ask you to consider when you look from behind the ball, your brain will see all it needs to see.

Remember when we discussed earlier the importance of quality questions, and how the quality of your life will be determined by the quality of your questions? Here is a great example. Your brain will work out the putt as long as you ask it one very specific question. As you look from behind the ball at the hole, I want you to ask: "What does this ball have to do to go in the hole?

Just think about that now: What does *this* ball have to *do* to go in the hole?

Given that our brains go to work on quality questions and good questions create good images, your brain will work out what the ball has to do in terms of line and speed. You may actually see the ball go in with an image in your mind, or you might just get a sense of what the ball needs to do. But, that question is so important because to work out the answer, your brain has to take into consideration *both* the line and the pace of the putt. It is a quality question that both focuses your attention and supplies your brain with quality information on which your subconscious mind can now go to work.

the mind factor

GET ON WITH IT!

Once you have asked this question and the answer has come to you (and it will if you ask the question with conviction), you now need to do all you can to hold this image in your mind's eye.

Remember! Golf is one of the very few sports we play where we are not actually looking where we are going. We have stated this before but it is important enough to repeat. In darts, you look at the board; in basketball you look at the hoop. But in golf, we are actually not looking at the target. So the next best thing is to have a very clear retained image of the target. Once you have asked the question and you have a clear line, it is very important you do not hang around and waste too much time – which can allow the image to fade.

I really like the idea you have your practice strokes (*if* you need them) from behind the ball, on the same line you read the putt. In effect, you are still looking down the line and seeing the same images as you saw when the question was asked.

Taking practice strokes from the side of the ball puts you on a different line and it gives you the opportunity to become too involved in the mechanics of the stroke.

Now it is time to step into the ball and what happens next is crucial.

DEVELOP A "QUIET EYE"

If you are serious about improving your putting, I would urge you to look at the work of Joan Vickers, a kinesiology professor (that's the study of human movement) at the University of Calgary – specifically her seminal work on what she calls "The quiet eye".

Poor putters have what she would call poor "gaze control". They look at the hole without really looking. They look at the ball without really looking at the ball; their eyes in effect send poor information to the brain. Good putters do the opposite. When they look at the hole, they *really* look – and they fixate on a point where the ball is going to enter the hole. They then track back along the line they have seen and then finally fixate on a *precise* spot on the back of the ball. Busy eyes create a busy and usually anxious brain.

Picture the classic scene of a nervous individual at an interview and how their eyes seem to dart all over the place, making themselves, and you, uncomfortable; as opposed to when you are sat across from perhaps a loved one and your eyes fix on them purposely but in a relaxed manner.

Ever since I became aware of this work, it felt like the final piece of a big puzzle for me. Over the years, I had seen golfers with a great routine get over the ball and then seemingly break down and not be able to hole putts with any consistency. When I began to check what their eyes were doing, almost inevitably they had very poor gaze control and their eyes just flicked about all over the place, breaking the quality of the picture that had been initially supplied by the *quality* question.

I suggest you become aware of this final piece of the jigsaw. Ideally ask someone to film what your eyes are doing when you get set over the ball. In an ideal world you should get into position, track the line of the putt slowly, fixate on a specific point where the ball will enter the hole and then come back to put your attention on a specific point on the back of the ball. Time and time again, when working with players, when this final piece is in place they begin to report how quiet eyes go along with a quiet mind and a much stronger sense of having done all they can to give themselves the best chance of holing the putt. Then simply let go, knowing all of the information the brain needs has been supplied, nothing more nothing less.

Fix that final gaze and then let the genius of your unconscious mind take over.

the mind factor

DEAL WITH IT

So what happens next?

You pull the trigger and the ball slips quietly into the middle of the hole? Wouldn't that be nice!

Part of developing the ideal mind set to become a great putter may seem somewhat negative. But the truth is a lot of putts you hit really well on seemingly the perfect line will not go in. This is an appropriate moment to re-affirm The Three Phases of Golf we met in Chapter Three.

In phase one, the Pre-Shot Phase, you have put into your system quality information. You have executed your Pre-Shot routine to the absolute best of your ability. You have stepped into the ball and you have focused your attention in a useful place. In Phase two, the Shot Phase, you have let go... but the ball missed!

This is where that vital third phase, the Post-Shot Phase, comes into its own. A 100% commitment to deal with the outcome is paramount. I see so many golfers miss a putt and buckle at the knees, groaning about how should a well-struck putt could possibly miss. This is a *really bad* question! It missed because that is what a lot of putts do!

The quality question to ask at this stage is: "Did I execute and commit to Phase One and Phase Two?" If you did, then you have done your bit. You have done all you can and that is all you should concern yourself with. As tough as this can be, if you commit to this totally, then you are again putting yourself into a state of mind that will, in the long run, allow you to hole as many putts as you possibly can.

If there is a secret to becoming a great putter then that is it, there and then. If you get to the point you are not afraid to miss because you will *deal with it*, then you have arrived at the point where you become fearless... and that frees you to hole as many putts as possible. In effect, you get out of your own way.

One suggestion I would offer in the Post-Shot Phase is to make sure that after every putt as you walk off the green, you momentarily place your attention on your breathing. Have the intention that this becomes just as much an important part of the routine than anything that may come before it. Once you place your attention on your breath, you are focused on the body which is in the here and now. You are not staying with the missed putt and all of the potential consequences of ifs, buts and maybes. You are staying in the present and you are dealing with the outcome. This isn't always easy, but as we have said all the way through this book, if you ignore the Post-Shot Phase, then don't be surprised if the first two Phases start to disappoint you.

When you have put all this together, you will end up with a wonderful formula that I call the Circle of Possibility.

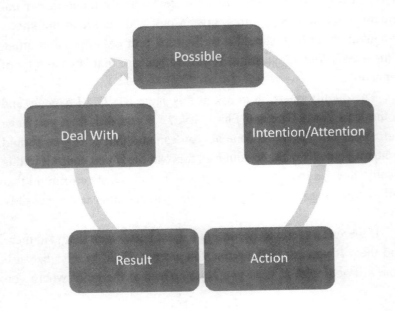

If you start with each putt from a mind set of "possible", then you are open to create a clear *intention*. That intention will focus your *attention* and hold your mind in a useful place. You then take an *action* – you move the putter back and through and there will be a *result*: the ball will either go in the hole or it won't. But if you commit to deal with the result, then you will find you are able to loop back to the next "possible". If you don't deal with it, your ability to see the "possible" closes down and you will not be able to create any clarity of intention or attention.

After a while of doing this, you will probably then start to blame your action and you then try to change this, or that, or your putter... and the insanity begins! This insanity then lasts anything between six rounds and 60 years depending on at what point you choose to adopt the Circle of Possibility.

As I have introduced this concept to many golfers over the years, a lot of them report back how this very simple formula has magical affect in almost any area of life. The core concepts of "Possible" and "Deal With" become a lifelong mantra that allows them to face a multitude of situations knowing they will get through, as long as they keep to the simple sequence of the Circle.

It is only a suggestion, but it may be worth thinking about where you can use this principle other than the obvious place on a putting green. I promise if you commit to this long term, you will be very pleasantly surprised.

CHAPTER 6

THE "CONE OF CONTENTION"

What does the name Tony Lema mean to you? Have you ever heard of him? Do you know anything about him?

Well, perhaps we *should* all know a little bit more about "Champagne Tony". This fascinating man, his tragic story and, in particular, his clear perception of what he believed, was key to his turning into a truly great golfer. I believe they provide a terrific insight into how *you* can achieve lower scores.

In 1964, Lema won the Open Championship at St Andrews. This was an unbelievable surprise. Lema was not only making his first appearance in the Open, but had only completed nine holes of practice before starting. However, Lema had hired Arnold Palmer's regular Open caddie, Tip Anderson, since Palmer was not competing that year. Anderson, a descendant of past Open Champion Jamie Anderson, had grown up on the course and, in all likelihood, knew more about it than anyone else. It proved an inspired decision; Lema won by five shots over Jack Nicklaus.

From 1963 through July 1966, Lema finished in the top 10 more than 50% of the time on the PGA Tour and never missed a cut in a major, finishing in the top 10 in 8 of the 15 Majors in which he played. He was a member of the 1963 and 1965 United States Ryder Cup teams, and his Ryder Cup record (9-1-1) is the best of any player who has played in two or more Ryder Cups.

In 1966, when Lema was 32, tragedy struck. He was flying with his wife, Betty from the PGA Championship at Firestone Country Club in Ohio, to an exhibition tournament – the Little Buick Open in Illinois – when their chartered twin-engine plane ran out of fuel and crashed in a water hazard near the 7th green of Lansing Country Club in Lansing, Illinois, very close to their destination. All four people on board were killed.

Who knows what Lema may have gone on to achieve; but golf undoubtedly lost one of its brightest stars that day.

Lema was renowned for his colourful social life and sense of fun, hence the "Champagne Tony" tag. But, he was clearly a man ahead of his time in terms of the way he looked at the game – long before extensive statistics on just about everything became the norm.

Lema used to talk about the "Cone of Contention". He defined this as the area from around 75 yards into the flag. This is where he believed the tournament was won or lost. He dedicated himself to learning distance control and feel for these shots, knowing that because he hit the ball a long way, his distance could only be turned into an advantage if his *short game* was good.

If you are one of the multitudes who have tried everything they can to hit it further – from spending a fortune on new technology to gym sessions to lessons – note this lesson well: added distance is only useful if you can take advantage of it with good pitching.

For me, Lema's focus on the Cone of Contention was central to his success. Becoming sharp from 75 yards in will have a massive positive influence on your scoring. It will also improve your ability to make a score when your swing is off. Just imagine being *really* good at getting the ball down in two shots from this range and the effect that will have on your game! You hit a poor tee shot, you leave your second well short of the green… but with your third shot, you go through your process and the ball zeroes in to about five feet and you hole the putt! You have made only a par, but at times a par can almost feel like an eagle. It can be the moment in a round where just one shot *can* make all the difference. As I mentioned in Chapter 4, it could well be argued that it was Luke Donald's outstanding ability in the Cone of Contention that allowed him to become World Number One.

Learn what you need to do to be better at pitching and, in particular, how to improve your distance control. To improve in this area obviously involves developing some technical skills; you need to have an action that can control the trajectory of the ball. Distance control is tough if you can't control the flight. Any investment and improvement you make in this area will be hugely rewarded. I would recommend you look to take some instruction on your action from someone who specialises in this area of the game.

That said, I want to present some ideas to you in terms of your approach to this part of the game which, I am certain, will reward you with almost instant score improvement if you commit to them.

FRAME OF MIND: GET TENACIOUS

We often hear labels given to people: "She has a stubborn streak," or "He is easily distracted". When we hear we have been given a label, in time, we often *become* that label. Many people are bad putters not just as a result of a less-than-perfect stroke, but because they take on the label of being a bad putter. They live it and they breathe it to the extent they start to believe it.

Just think for a moment all of the "labels" you carry around with you. Perhaps you were told at school you weren't musical; or if you were lucky, you had a teacher tell you that you were "sporty". We become the labels others give us. We create a self-fulfilling prophecy. If we can create our own labels, we can guide ourselves towards the qualities we want to possess.

I want you to consider that you could perhaps give yourself *new* label that could be useful to you in the future – that, in doing so, you could create a new *persona* for yourself. You decide what kind of person you want to be as opposed to being told by others. The principle of "Act as if" has been around in the world of psychology for a long time. "Fake it until you make it" is a term embedded in popular culture.

Experience proves to us that, with the right approach, this can be done. Richard Bandler, the co-developer of neuro-linguistic programming, once told a shy person to *pretend* to be confident. "I know you can't be confident," he said. "But I would just like you to pretend you are." The linguistic genius of this is that a person *pretending* to be confident is not bound by his past conditioning. He is just pretending.

A number of years ago, a British TV channel ran a series called *Faking It*. People were plucked from their regular environment and given just four weeks to take on a completely different persona and then fool a panel of experts. You would see people meet challenges they should have been completely ill-suited for. One, in particular, was a chap called Maxim who was extremely shy. He was a chess champion, with an IQ of more than 170, very introverted. He tended to just be at home on his own and he shunned contact with the outside world. His challenge was to become a football coach! He was thrown literally into the tough macho world of Brentford FC. The coach there was a very abrasive say-it-as-you-see-it type.

At first, Maxim was clearly extremely uncomfortable and out of place. He wanted to give in; everything in his system told him to leave and return to his "normal" persona. His past conditioning told him he was a cerebral chess champion who would never cut it in this alien world. Yet, he hung in there, he absorbed himself in his new world, his new context and, slowly but surely, he took it on and became a different person.

During the series, it was always fascinating to watch just how many people managed to fool the experts because they had immersed themselves in a new label. They had "become" something different as a result of shedding their past conditioning. Maxim himself didn't manage to fool the judges but you could see what it had meant to him personally; he had proved himself able to make new friends and be

the mind factor

part of a world a couple of weeks previously was totally alien to his personality.

We don't *have* to be fixed by our past conditioning. Personality doesn't have to be fixed; we can decide to become someone different than the current story we carry around with us. Yes, to change can feel uncomfortable, but if you fight through those feelings, what emerges on the other side is very liberating. To see that we, as human entities, are essentially made up of a bunch of stories. This is a great metaphor, because we can actively choose to write a new script.

The attitude you employ when you get into the Cone of Contention is vital. And with this in mind, I suggest the label you give yourself in this area is *tenacious*. The dictionary definitions of tenacious as: *holding together, cohesive, not easily pulled asunder, tough.* You are not easily pulled asunder; you hold things together... things like a golf score, for instance.

Imagine now if you went onto a golf course and you pretended to be tenacious in the Cone of Contention. What would that look like? How would that feel? How would you respond if you had played a hole badly and you were left with a 60-yard pitch into a tight pin? How would you talk to yourself if you were tenacious? If you pretended to be tenacious, what would you put your attention on?

Being tenacious would mean that you found a way of getting the ball around the course when you were less than a 100% on your game. You would become a very tough and frustrating opponent for others to try to beat – and your confidence would sky rocket.

HOW TO BECOME SKILLED
IN THE "CONE OF CONTENTION"

Do the following drill over the next few weeks. If you are a professional, it will make you a lot of money; if you are an amateur, it will bring your handicap tumbling down. It is similar to a drill I believe Luke Donald spent a lot of time working with as he marched to the World no 1 spot in 2011.

To do this drill, you need to invest in a range finder. Once you have that, I want you to go to an area where you can pitch at a flag with 10 balls. Start from any position from 75 yards to 30 yards. Follow this process:

1. Stand and look at the distance. Try to gauge it in your mind – 45 yards, 47 yards, go on make a guess.

2. Now use the range finder and find out exactly what the distance is. How close did you get? Not very, if you are like most people. This is going to be important later.

Now, the drill is this on each shot:

1. Guess the distance. Say it out loud to commit to your guess.
2. Actually get the distance from your range finder.
3. Feel the shot with a practice swing.
4. Play the shot.
5. Note if the shot is within that magic 6ft area, and mark down the result.
6. Move on to the next random distance.

Do this with 10 balls and record how many shots are within 6ft. Very quickly you will begin to get an average for this. Just by improving your average by one on this game, you are statistically more likely to reduce your score on the course.

Can you begin to imagine how good this drill can make you... not just at estimating the distance accurately, but then – more importantly – being able to hit the correct distance with just *one* opportunity?

I am being deadly serious when I say if you have the discipline to do this two to three times a week, you will elevate your game to a level of scoring you didn't think possible.

This for me, is the crown jewel of all the practice games I have used over the years. Just 15 minutes, three times a week. Do you think that might be worthwhile doing if it were to have such a big impact on your game and possibly your career?

What this game will give you out on the course is two very powerful scoring assets. First, it will give you the chance to make a score when you are not swinging your best; and second, if your ball striking is on and you are driving close to a short Par 4s or getting close to Par 5s in two, you will go on to make a stack of birdies.

I always talk to players in terms of the value of *one* shot and what that can do for a career, a championship or just a club handicap. I am absolutely certain if you look into the wisdom of the late Tony Lema, you will be very pleasantly surprised at how much of a return you get on your investment of time and effort in this specific area.

CHAPTER 7

HOW TO MAKE YOUR PRACTICE COUNT

We have already talked about how to build a better golf swing by having your attention in the right place and structuring your practice to get the best out of your time on the range. We have discussed how vitally important it is to get out and *play* golf on a golf course. But I am also aware that for a variety of reasons, many of you will still spend a good portion of your time on the range. With this in mind, I want to run through some thoughts, suggestions and ideas that will really maximise the effectiveness of your practice.

It is amazing that so many golfers will say the game is 90% mental, yet when you then ask them what they are doing about training the mental side of the game, they will look at you with a puzzled expression. I have to say a lot of people think working on your mental game is about sitting with a set of headphones on listening to affirmations or sitting cross legged visualising the perfect round. Those things *can* have some impact, but I have to say in my experience, that impact is limited because it is extremely difficult to get most people to stick with it in any long-term way. Remember our old friends Context and Environment? We met them in Chapter 4. We must understand that to practise the challenges of the mental game, we probably need to be in a context or an environment the brain recognises as being similar to the environment in which we are going to be put to the test. I am not poo-pooing visualisation and imagery, as there is well-documented evidence to suggest that it can help; but rather than going just with the mind, it is much easier and more productive to structure your actual *physical* practice to contain an element of *mental* training.

This type of practice has, I believe, three important components which make up what I have come to call the Practice Pyramid:

Let us evaluate each of those three elements in turn, and look at how one factor melds into the next.

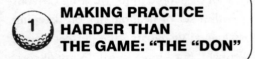

MAKING PRACTICE HARDER THAN THE GAME: "THE "DON""

In 2005 I was asked to do a series of seminars on the **MIND FACTOR** by the Australian PGA. As it happened, for an Englishman traveling to Australia to discuss mental toughness, it was perfect and fortunate timing, as that year the England cricket team had finally wrestled the precious Ashes from their Aussie counterparts after the best part of 20 years. And, even more fortunately, I'd had the honour of working with the then-England Captain Michael Vaughan on his own game during that series.

During one of the legs of the trip, I was hosted by a cricket fanatic called Geoff Ranenburg. He told me he had the pleasure of meeting the greatest batsman of all time, the legendary Australian Sir Donald Bradman. Bradman, I believe, actually has possession of *the* greatest statistic in the whole of sport. If you are a batsman in cricket,

the mind factor

then you have what is known as a "batting average' – a simple run average which constitutes a reflection of your overall batting ability in your career to date. If as a batsman you average around 50 at test match level, then you are in a tiny minority of the *very* best. Bradman had a test average spanning over twenty years of 99.94 – absolutely off the scale. The next best in the history of the game is around the 60 mark.

To clarify that, of *all* the people who have *ever* played cricket, the best is around 60. And then you have the Don, who averaged 99.94! It would have been more than 100 if he'd managed to score four runs or more in his last innings, instead of the duck (zero runs) he got.

Anyway, Ranenburg shared with me a story about Bradman on which I have since done some research. Apparently, all through his career, Bradman used to practise with a cricket stump and a golf ball. He would throw the ball at a wall and then defend it with the stump. He said that by doing this, it helped him to focus intently; but it also gave him the perception that when he played the real game with a bigger bat and a bigger ball, the game seemed easier.

The key learning here is that Bradman was making a *portion* of his practice more difficult than the game. It is something that is very common in other sports. Top-class basketball players practise with a smaller hoop; sprinters run with a parachute attached to their back. Apparently, the greatest footballer of all time, Pele, used to practise his skills with an orange. In Brazil, they don't learn to play football first, they learn to play a game called Futsal, which is played in a smaller area and is **FASTER** than the real game.

These "games" are, in effect, making a part of your practice more difficult than the actual game. This practice does not just refine and sharpen skills – it also employs the mental technique of shaping your perception of the challenge, in order to make the real game seem easier.

All sports seem to understand this technique other than one. The way we practise golf actually achieves the opposite. We stand there on a wide open field and smash balls into the distance... and then wonder why the real game, on that tree-lined, lake-strewn course, seems so difficult. I would strongly recommend you take time to consider how you could make a part of your practice more difficult than the game. Not all of it; just a portion that can help you shape your perception so the actual game begins to seem easier. Here are four ways to do just that:

10 CHANCE

Gather 10 balls on the range. Create a 25 yard-wide "fairway", using markers and/or your imagination. Your aim is simply to try to get as many of the 10 drives within the 25-yard markers. Make it your goal to get seven out of 10 or better with the area.

You only get one chance at this; but if you achieve the goal, then play the game again this time with a 20-yard fairway. If you achieve 7 out of 10, again you reduce the "fairway" some more.

You can use this principle with any club. The twin keys are (i) you only get one chance per set of 10 and (ii) every time you succeed, the next test is harder. Just imagine how this could affect your perception if you get used to finding fairways that are really narrow? When you get out onto the course, the normal fairway then seems much wider. This is why I believe 10 Chance should become a staple part of your practice.

NEEDLE PUTTING

The phrases we use on good putting days have always fascinated me. "The hole seemed like a bucket" is one, vividly describing that in the mind of someone holing a lot of putts, the perception is that the hole is large. Of course, the hole never changes size, but our perception of it obviously does. Surely then, a part of your practice should be geared to shaping this perception?

the mind factor

I used to get people practising their putting to a tee peg from around 10 feet, but now I think a tee is far too big! I want you to find a large needle and then spray it white. Then, take it onto the putting green and practise from short range with one ball to this tiny target. You will be pleasantly surprised at how many times you manage to strike the needle.

When you then putt to a hole, you can actually position the needle at the back of the hole. Again, you will be pleasantly surprised at the apparent size the hole now takes on. The other beauty of this drill is that you spend less time seeing yourself missing the hole. There is no negative association attached to missing the needle but a huge positive if you actually hit it – the opposite of what we normally achieve with standard putting practice to a regular cup.

SMALLER-HEADED CLUBS

I am not really much in favour of many of the teaching gadgets out there as they can never be used in the context of the golf course; but I do like the smaller-headed clubs widely available. When you practise for a short while with a very small-headed putter or a small-headed iron, it is amazing just how well you tend to strike the ball when you go back to standard-sized clubs. Here is a direct link with the Don and how he practised with the golf ball and cricket stump.

WORST BALL

I have already described the importance of Worst Ball in Chapter 4, but here I want to restate the point, as I think it is such a vitally important practice concept. When you constantly have to make a successful shot twice to progress, it makes the normal game *seem* so much easier when you only have to strike one iron shot, or hole the putt once, to make your score.

Vary all of these games. They will make your practice not only more interesting and challenging but also *much* more productive.

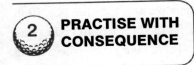

2 PRACTISE WITH CONSEQUENCE

If you take a direct comparison between golf and some other sports, we can easily come up with some interesting distinctions. Let's take football as an example. A world famous striker has two great chances to score in the first half but misses both; in the second half he scores a goal and his team wins 1-0. What would everybody remember? The goal or his mistakes?

A tennis player sends a serve out of court and what happens? He gets another go at the serve. A cricketer bowls five awful balls in an over but then takes a wicket with the sixth. What do people remember? Yet, if Lee Westwood is five-under-par after 14 holes during the first round of the Open Championship but he then manages to take a 10 on the 15th, what do you think people would remember?

The point I am making here is that golf is a tough game because *every* shot we hit on the course has a direct consequence to the score. We make contact with the ball and it goes on the card. In fact even if we miss the ball, it goes on the card! Yet, does that level of consequence get reflected in the way that we practise? Ball after ball fired into the blue yonder with little or no consequence? Then we go out onto the course and play the *ultimate* game of consequence.

Sian Beilock, from the University of Chicago, wrote the wonderful book *Choke* and has spent the greater part of her academic life analysing why we don't perform well under pressure. Beilock advises that we need to look closely at our practice habits and make sure a portion of the practice has the capability to "immunise" us from pressure by simulating the effects of consequence.

How do we simulate consequence in golf? Simply by taking into consideration that we are all generally our own biggest critic – and none of us likes to do badly where a test is involved.

One of the most basic but important investments you can ever make, I have named after my all-time favourite TV detective, Co-

the mind factor

lumbo! Those of you unfortunate, like me, to be old enough to re-member Columbo, will all recall he always had three things with him – a dirty old raincoat, a cigar and a pocket notebook. I don't need you to go out and buy either a raincoat or a cigar to improve your golf; but I *do* need you to go out and buy a small pocket notebook. This notebook, I believe, will be one of the single most important pieces of equipment you will ever purchase for your game.

On every hole during a round of golf, you have to take out of your back pocket a piece of card; and you have to write down how many times you have just hit the ball. Yet, in practice, we *never* take time to record what we have just done. Imagine a snooker player playing a practice session with someone and never bothering to keep the score!

The very act of playing a game in practice and then having to take out the notebook, creates our all-important level of conse-quence. By having a score, we instantly create some pressure: maybe not as much as the real game, but enough to make practice more real to the brain, relative to the game itself.

Here are a couple of suggestions as to what type of games you should play, where you can add consequence via a scoring test. But in both, the principle is the key: play a game with *one* ball from a *unique* location and you keep the score.

PAR 18

Par 18 is simply one ball played from around the practice short game area. Pick nine different locations; each one represents a par-2 of a chip and a putt. So, you have a nine-hole, par-18 "course". Make sure you play three easy, three medium and three difficult shots. Play the shot onto the green, hole out with your putter and then move on to the next hole. You play all nine and then add up the score.

This is my all-time favourite and a game that, since I invented it 10 or more years ago, I have introduced to many players. US Open Champion Graeme McDowell has been kind enough to say it has been one of the most important aspects to our work together over the past eight years.

A variation on the game is Bunker 18, where you play nine different bunker shots. If you are at an advanced level, you can also make Par 18 more difficult: play the game with one ball and, if you shoot lower than 20, play again with two balls and take your *worst* score.

JUST 9

Play this on the putting green, again with one ball. Play three short putts from around 6ft, three medium putts from 6-20ft and three putts 20ft or longer. Strike the putts in a random order. Never play the short ones first and move onto the medium. Record your score. Remember, golf is a *random* game; we need to practise it as such, instead of always playing in a fixed and linear fashion.

3 BASE YOUR PRACTICE ON FACTS, NOT FEELINGS

Imagine if you were a 100 metre runner and in the middle of your training season for the Olympics, your coach informed you you were now going to take part in a training programme that had *no* stopwatch. He also insisted you trained on your own. Each day you trained, your coach told you that you were getting better. He filled you full of the *feeling* of confidence. Yet, now comes the

the mind factor

point where you are on the start line at the Olympics, lining up against a bunch of other athletes who you knew were regularly breaking 10 seconds. How would you feel if you had been told you were good but you had no way of knowing? The feelings you had from the words your coach gave you would evaporate like smoke from a kettle.

It sounds illogical and insane, yet this is the way we have gone about improvement at golf. I can think back to my own time, spending countless hours on the range. I would often hit the ball well and leave the range full of confidence. Yet, it would only take a couple of wild shots on the course for all of those good feelings to disappear. Feelings are fleeting – they come and go. Facts about your game give you something a little more robust to hold on to.

If you practise in the way I am describing here – keeping score – you will then take advantage of the final part of the practice pyramid. You will create facts, not feelings, to take to the course.

Let's say you play Par 18 and your first score is 32. After being told by your coach how very good players score less than 20 on a regular basis, you know your chipping is poor. However, you stick at the practice, you play Par 18 three times a week, you do some work on your technique and your understanding of loft and how to control trajectory. A number of weeks later you now are scoring in the mid 20s at Par 18. Based on that statistic, are you more or less likely to get it up-and-down more often on the course? You *know* you are – and your new-found confidence is now based on something a little more substantial than feelings and the words of someone else.

I guarantee that if you apply yourself to this form of practice for a sustained period of time you, *will* be more confident and you will see results... because you have trained your brain as well as your body.

THE POWER OF PERSEVERANCE

Some of the above is a departure from the norm, but it is a way of practising which will produce results if you want to lower your scores. This is a presupposition I have made, considering the fact you are reading this book. If you love to practise by smashing balls down the range and working on perfecting your swing gives you great pleasure, then please do not change that. Part of the game of golf is knowing exactly what you and you alone want from it. If it is lower scores and a reduced handicap or an increase in your tournament winnings, then the Practice Pyramid is worth the time and effort.

I can promise you it is *not* easy. It may take less time but you will find it infinitely more frustrating and challenging than the way you currently practise. You will have the part of your brain that loves familiarity tugging at you to go back to the hit-and-scrape you have done in the past.

If you are ready for the challenge, though, if you are prepared to deal with the frustration, you will come out the other side knowing you have improved as a golfer as opposed to that hollow speculation you might be. There is a world of difference between the two, and when you get onto the golf course, you will feel it. If you've chosen that fact-based route, you will experience the joy of playing with a deeper-rooted confidence – and you will find yourself much better equipped to produce the results you want.

CHAPTER 8

GOLF'S "THINKING SINS"

During my years working in the field of golf and golf performance, I have observed that in certain areas of the mind game, golfers are repeat offenders. In this chapter, I want to share with you some ideas on what I've chosen to call "The Thinking Sins".

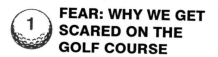

FEAR: WHY WE GET SCARED ON THE GOLF COURSE

I had a fascinating conversation a few years ago with a Golf Professional called Kim Larssen who was working with Fred Shoemaker at the Extraordinary Golf School. Kim is based in the most beautiful of places – Carmel Valley, near to Pebble Beach. He is no ordinary coach and his life experiences are something special to listen to.

He is a Vietnam War veteran and some of the things he saw on the battlefield as a 19-year-old made me shudder. To see a number of close friends killed right in front of him must have created painful memories that for the rest of us, who have never experienced anything like it, cannot comprehend. When I asked him how long he had been in Vietnam, his reply told it all: "I have been in Vietnam for the past 30 years."

On his return from Vietnam, Kim got into coaching golf. During our chat, he told me one of the things that puzzled him after his life experiences was the amount of *fear* people have on a golf course. Hearing people talk about being "scared" of a putt or a chip shot was something that, to this man, seemed somewhat strange. To have been on a battlefield would, I suspect, put a delicate chip over a bunker into some kind of perspective.

Reflecting many years later on that conversation, I began to think of all the strange things we all get scared of in life – things that are actually never going to bring any *real* harm to us.

I myself am no different. I could list a whole host of things from opening tee shots to public speeches that shouldn't be an issue for me... but they are! Certainly from my experience of working with players over the years, it could well be said that the real problem in golf is not so much slices or shanks, but the fear of them that we all bring with us to the golf course.

Fear breeds tension; and tension has a huge negative impact on our swing in terms of rhythm and balance. Swings that work just fine on the range go to pieces on the golf course. What on earth is going on? And, more importantly, what can we begin to do about it?

With these concepts in mind, it was great to read a terrific book on the subject, *Nerve*, by Taylor Clark. In the book, Clark explains in a very engaging style how it is not so much the fear that is the problem but our reaction to it. In a nutshell, he argues, our brain is designed so that fear is a natural survival mechanism, hard wired into us over ancient millennia to help us stay alive.

Clark backs this up with science. It is the job of a small almond-shaped section of our brain, called the amygdala, to warn us about potentially dangerous situations. In the days when we lived in caves, the amygdala would "tag" a certain experience such as a particular predator and make sure we avoided that situation in the future in order to survive.

The problem with this inherently useful part of our brain is that, today, it is mostly redundant. There are not many situations in our everyday life that compare with having to contend with a sabre-toothed tiger's intention to have us for lunch. Yet the amygdala still tags what it perceives as threatening situations even if in reality that situation will not kill or even harm us.

So, that pitch over a bunker will not harm us; but the potential for failure will get tagged as a threat to our sense of self and the amygdala goes into full swing, getting us all worked up and ready to either run away of fight it. Neither course of action is particularly useful for a soft lob over a trap!

The brain is creating an inappropriate response to a modern situation, and you can rest assured your brain and mine will keep giving that response. The real key is what we do in reply to the brain's over-sensitivity and how we calm down the amygdala.

In *Nerve,* Taylor Clark makes a number of valid suggestions on how to deal with our fears based on the latest neuroscientific research. Deceptively simple, they give us a roadmap of how to deal with these fears that have such a negative impact on our game. It is well worth reading the book, but here are my three favourites:

BREATHE

When we get fearful, our breathing changes – and that actually makes the problem worse. We encountered the benefits of deep breathing in Chapter 3, on how it helps us release in the Pre-Shot Phase. But deep breaths from the diaphragm also fight fear by calming the amygdala down and essentially "re-setting" its reaction.

As much as we may know this information, the key is to *do* it. A parent of a young player once told me that he was a little bit disappointed I had worked with his son on effective breathing as part of his Pre-Shot routine. He was disappointed, he said, because the lad had "heard it before". I could only explain that there is a big difference between knowing something and doing it. Quite frankly, his son was not doing it.

This state of affairs is far from unique: you may have heard about the importance of breathing and the way it calms our system down as well; yet, have you actually integrated it into your golfing system? Do you utilise the power of effective breathing in between shots?

Every golfer finds themselves fretting about what may or may not happen for the rest of the round at some point. All that time would be put to much better use if you used it to focus on dampening down that overactive amygdala.

This is not something I *think* works. It does work – and in far more testing situations than on a golf course. US Army psychologist Dave Grossman teaches his students to use the following breathing exercise on the battlefield:

1. Slowly draw the air in through your nose down into your abdomen for four leisurely counts (place your hand on your stomach to make sure your belly expands when you inhale)

2. Hold for four counts then exhale through your mouth for four counts. Hold again for four counts and repeat as necessary.

This simple but effective exercise could have so many benefits if you choose to use it in between shots. It can help you release the tension which may have built up as a result of some bad shots and allow you to let go of harmful and toxic anger.

It could help you deal with the possibility of being in contention and feeling under pressure. As you are coming down the stretch, if you are thinking about the fact you have a chance to win, then your mind has escaped to a potential future scenario. Ground yourself in the present moment by bringing your attention to your breathing.

the mind factor

It is simple but centuries-old old wisdom that can have the biggest effect on our game and, above all, it can allow us to get back a sense of perspective about the game of golf.

Yes, the *game* of golf.

Kim Larssen said to me he was amazed how many people he coached had ceased to see golf as a game. They created a perspective in their mind it was something so important that it was worth getting really scared about. Not for one minute am I saying golf isn't important, or your score isn't important: but what is also important is your ability to see golf through the kind of perspective which allows you to be the best golfer that you can be.

Good golf needs to be allowed out. It cannot be forced. And when you allow yourself to play golf as a game and you see it for what it really is, the golfer who lurks inside of you, and all his true potential, can finally be released.

CONFRONT DISCOMFORT

Put yourself under pressure in practice. Do not just hit balls. This will *not* cure your fears. Exposure to pressure is what makes you immune to it. This is an absolute priority if you intend to play the game at the highest level.

Most of us avoid the situations that scare us. This is the *single* biggest factor in making the pathways of fear stronger. As we have already said, the way our brains are wired, we create lots and lots of inappropriate fear in the modern world. Fear stops us becoming the best that we can be.

Perversely, many people are happy to confront fear in ways that offer no practical benefit, like jumping off bridges attached to a rubber band; but they will avoid areas in their life that would make a significant difference to the quality of their experience if they would only open up and face their fear.

Jumping off a bridge is not an inherently useful skill. Nor is throwing yourself out of a plane when it is not broken. But standing up in public and giving a presentation, or hitting a great shot off the first tee, are. Yet, if the fear is there and we don't confront it and quieten the amygdala, then come the end of our days, we are going to look back and have a lot of "if only's" and there will come a point for us all when there are no more rounds to play. Do you want the possibility of some great experiences to be taken away from you because you failed to confront your irrational and debilitating fears?

The concept of immunisation is a very powerful one in the sense that if you can expose yourself to a little bit of pressure in practice, if you can put yourself in a position where you feel uneasy, then you will gradually build up that fearlessness which comes from the exposure to the thing you thought was such a big problem.

Just consider now, how you could begin to put yourself in uncomfortable situations you have previously avoided with your golf. Think of things on a scale of nought (no discomfort) to 10 (massive discomfort). What are the situations in the game that would have you shaking with fear? First tee? Coming down the stretch? An easy three-footer?

Now set up situations in practice that may be just two or three on that scale. It may be a friend watching you; it may be keeping a score; it may be trying a difficult shot or shots that you normally avoid.

Seek out the discomfort. The more you do this, the more you are really making a difference to what will be reflected out on the course. If you are practising and your comfort level is at zero or one, then you are not really practising golf, you are practising in a way that will have limited effects on your fears and anxieties.

Move that up a notch and you will be doing yourself and your game a serious favour. It will also help to engage your brain in the third fear-beating principle we will address.

ABSORB YOURSELF IN THE PROCESS, NOT THE SITUATION

Our brain loves the idea of *knowing* what will happen. This is why most of our fears exist in the future. We project into the future and negatively predict what *may* happen. A few are influenced by what has happened in the past but it is our perception of an *imaginary* outcome that is the key to our fears.

Most of our predictions will not come true. Good or bad, there are just too many variables to our existence to predict almost anything accurately. But it is our fixation with the ability to predict what will happen that causes most of our uncertainty.

I am often amazed at the popularity of psychics, mystics and fortune tellers. You may or may not be a believer but it is incredible to me how people will go to such great lengths to try to predict the future, when we are not even that good at predicting what the weather will do tomorrow – let alone who we may or may not meet in the future!

The utter incompetence of so-called "experts" when it comes to predicting the future is well documented in many areas, though most notably in the financial world, when it comes to predicting what will happen in the markets in the future. It has been shown how monkeys throwing darts at a board of stocks and shares can have roughly the same efficacy as the so-called gurus. It reminds me of the great quote about there being two types of market prediction analysts – those who don't know, and those who don't know they don't know.

What is the antidote to all of this incredible desire to predict the future and tie ourselves in such an emotional mess?

Instead of focusing on the situation, focus on your *process*. I have talked about this extensively in Chapter 3, but it stands reiterating here: your routine is your life raft under pressure. Get one, work on it and trust it.

When we become absorbed in the process of what we are doing, we are keeping our mind in the place that even the first grade psychology books will tell you to be in – the present moment. We cannot control the outcome of a golf shot any more than we can control the outcome of a tournament. The minute the ball and the club meet each other, there will always be an element of unpredictability: remember, even the perfect putt on the perfect line at the perfect pace does *not* necessarily go in the hole.

We do, though, have control over and can totally influence our process. Process puts your focus on the present, and gives you the best chance of success. This is science telling us the importance of The Three Phases of Golf.

These three concepts contain some really simple ideas that do work. But the underlying message comes through loud and clear: if you want to deal with your fears, you need to face them. Avoidance only strengthens that inappropriate brain response.

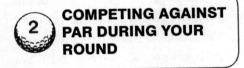

2 COMPETING AGAINST PAR DURING YOUR ROUND

I vividly remember having another conversation with 2010 US Open Champion Graeme McDowell about his putting. He had noticed that for a number of weeks that, if he had a putt for par in the 6-10ft range, he would more often than not hole it. Yet, if the putt was from the same distance for birdie, he would tend not to convert it. He felt everything he did was the same: he approached the putts the same

the mind factor

way, yet the results were poles apart. I would guess a lot of you may have experienced something similar over the years.

It never ceases to amaze me how golf can throw at you the most illogical and quirky statistics, the likes of which have no place in logical analysis. As we all know, from the minute you hit your first tee shot to the point where you hole your final putt, each and every shot counts exactly the same. A golf shot is a golf shot! Yet, it would seem we do better on certain shots than others.

Let's look again at those two scenarios McDowell faced – and that we all confront every time we play a game of golf. In the first, we have a putt to *avoid* a bogey; in the second, we have a putt to *gain* a birdie. Which do you think we would execute more successfully?

Economists David Pope and Maurice Schweitzer at the University of Pennsylvania analysed more than 2.5 million such putts in detail to see if there would be any difference in the results. And those results were fascinating in that at almost every distance, the conversion to *save* par was statistically better than the conversion to *gain* a birdie!

Why is that?

One possible explanation for this is something called "Loss Aversion". Noted psychologist Daniel Kahneman has written extensively about this and the fact most humans will do far more to avoid loss than move towards gain. Loss aversion theory tells us that, in effect, it seems to our human mind it is more painful to lose £100 than the equivalent balance of pleasure in winning £100. Avoiding pain appears more valuable to us than gaining pleasure.

Could it be we subconsciously focus differently when we are faced with the possibility of "losing" a par as opposed to "gaining" a birdie? That we somehow work harder to avoid the loss than to secure the gain? It sounds totally counterintuitive but it is something I have seen time and time again with players of all levels of the game.

These unconscious drivers of our behaviour shouldn't have such a powerful pull – but they do.

Loss aversion could perhaps also explain how we feel so uncomfortable when we get to a point in the round when we are under par or playing below our handicap. Again, do we subconsciously want to "hold on to what we have" a bit more than we want to go lower and shoot a seriously good score? It is almost universal. We all have scores we are comfortable with and when we start to look as though we can shoot lower than that, we want to hang on to that comfortable outcome. We don't tend to keep pushing forwards and riding the wave of our excellent play.

What can you do about this? How can you avoid the mysterious and rather unhelpful drive that is loss aversion?

The very heart of the problem of loss aversion at golf – but also of its solution – is the trap of thinking we are either under or over par while we are still playing our round of golf. This is something we have been subconsciously conditioned into thinking about from an early age. For me, it is the biggest culprit and is something you see on all golf broadcasts. Something which is telling you a blatant *lie*. I call this the "Myth of the Leaderboard".

Picture it now. Up on your screen flashes some information that says something along the lines of :

Mickelson:	-9	18 Holes
Westwood:	-9	12 Holes
Donald:	-9	15 Holes

Now, when you look at these phenomena closely, you may realise how you have been conned into thinking something is real when, in fact, it isn't. Who is the *only* player who is *actually* under par?

Mickelson, of course, is the only one who is actually under par because he has finished his round, signed his card and is in the clubhouse. The other two, Donald and Westwood, are not actually under par because they can't decide to stick at that score and walk in to the clubhouse after 12 or 15 holes.

We are looking at the illusion of being under par or having *any* form of score while we are actually still playing. Yet, this perceived ownership of being under par can be taken away in an instant.

This doesn't happen with other sports. In Football, if you score a goal, if you are winning 1–0 with ten minutes to go, then you may or may not end up winning the game itself – but that goal you have scored can never be taken away from you. It's in the bank. Once you have scored a run at cricket, it cannot be unscored. But with golf your current score is nothing more than an illusion. To repeat, you do not *own* your score! You just think you do. Then, when the dynamic of loss aversion kicks in, even the best players in the world don't want to lose what they perceive they own.

If you can rid yourself of this illusion or delusion, as the case may be, then you will find yourself free to play without the spectre of loss aversion kicking in. After all, when you grasp your score relative to par is an illusion, you have nothing to lose.

Make a firm commitment you will *never* again say "I was three under after 14" or "I was five under with three to play"… or even "I was five under my handicap". No! You were not! You didn't "own" your score because you were still out on the course. You only own a score at golf when you have signed your card and you are in the clubhouse.

Commit to this totally and you will remove and eliminate one of the major golfing mental errors the game can throw at you.

Golf is a series of separate and unrelated tasks. You start with your first task on the first tee and you only run out of tasks when you finish up on the last. The cliché of one shot at a time is perhaps the greatest of mental skills to learn. And learning means you have to question how you have been programmed and brainwashed into believing certain things like "being under par". To eliminate this faulty thinking from your game is to separate you from the rest and gives you a huge advantage out on the course.

Here is a game that helps you avoid loss aversion and is a kind of bridge to get to the point where you play each and every shot on its merit. It's a game I believe Rory McIlroy played whilst blasting the field away in the 2011 US Open, and it's called Super 6.

Super 6 is the concept of playing golf not as two sets of nine holes which make up 18 but to play six sets of *three* holes. The goal very simply is to do as well as you can and score as low as possible on each and every set of three.

The beauty of this game is it also allows you to tap into another phenomenon that the human brain likes, which is the idea of "starting again". We love to set out goals and resolutions on the 1st January because we feel it is a new and fresh start. When you play Super 6, you are constantly giving yourself a fresh start and it moves you in the direction of being able to play one hole at a time.

Above all else though, never again fall into the trap of believing you are either under or over par while you are on the golf course. You are not! If you think you are, try walking in and seeing how valid your score actually is!

3 PERFECTIONISM

It is an interesting thought to consider that all mental strengths, taken to an extreme, can become a liability. I think perfectionism is definitely in that category.

The dictionary defines perfectionism as *a personal standard, attitude, or philosophy that demands perfection and rejects anything less.* To have elements in your personality that are perfectionistic can be a terrific quality. Certain professions lend themselves to

the mind factor

the need to be perfectionistic. I would like to think if you were going to build a bridge over a river that will have thousands of people travelling over it every day, then a strong element of perfectionism would be a good thing. If you have been prescribed life-saving medication and you have to take it every day, then again, being perfectionistic about that would, in the long run, be a pretty good thing.

Over the years, though, with the game of golf, I have seen too many talented players never fulfilling their potential because their perfectionism, and the way they applied it to their golf game, became devastating – to such a degree that the game they once loved becomes an absolute torture.

The problem with perfectionism in golf is that, taken to an extreme in the wrong areas, it can make you very miserable indeed. You become barely satisfied if you absolutely nail one where you aimed. Your best leaves you just about satisfied and well, anything less is totally unacceptable.

Dr Bob Rotella famously wrote a book many years ago called *Golf is Not a Game of Perfect*. I would agree with him, but with one caveat: I believe there are certain parts of your golf where you *can* be close to perfect most of the time. Other parts are not perfectible – and if you try, then you risk disaster. The real skill, then, is in identifying which areas you can be perfectionistic about which areas you will need to cut yourself some slack. Only then will you begin to play a game you will truly enjoy being part of.

I believe the way we have practised golf over the years, honing an "ideal" technique on the range as we have already discussed, breeds a fertile ground for inappropriate perfectionism. To stand on a range blasting 5-irons from a flat lie to an open field, will fuel perfectionism because you get an unrealistic perspective on the game. It is too easy and creates false expectation; you think you are better than you are.

If you have a tendency towards perfectionism, you'd do well to consider that in any single golf shot in the game, you have a few constants and a few variables. The constants are that your ball will always be at point A and you desire the ball to go to point B. This starts on the first tee and this equation only ends on the 18th hole.

From point A to point B, there will be a distance and a direction to consider in how to move from one point to another. There will be a decision as to the tool you are going to use for the task that confronts you. You will step into the shot, and you will send commands to your body to move the club. The club will generate some speed and some force, the two will meet each other and then they will separate.

The club could be travelling in excess of a 100mph and, if the face is open or closed by a fraction of a degree, then the ball will *not* travel to point B. If you are lucky, it will be to either C or D; but in some extreme cases it could be G and H! A tiny mis-application of force to that golf ball can send the thing miles off line.

The obvious point I am making here is that the odds of you hitting the ball *exactly* as you want to do are minuscule. Golf is a game of missing and failing. Accepting this is the first move to sidestepping inappropriate perfectionism.

However, you can attain a degree of perfection in what you do *before* you let the ball and club meet each other, because you have control over what you do.

My experience in the game is that most golfers are horribly un-perfectionistic about what they do *before* the shot, and then horrendously over-perfectionistic about the shot itself.

If you are beginning to recognise yourself here, you need to regain the balance on this. The key is to get yourself in a state of mind that allows you to be the best you can be.

I would want you to be perfectionistic in gathering what I would call *quality information*. To be able to say you have given a particular shot 100%, then you need to be able to say you inputted quality information into your onboard computer. This doesn't mean taking forever over a shot, but it does mean having the discipline to do what great players do.

It might feel to you I am stating something of the obvious. But you would be surprised how even with top level players, when they talk to me about poor outcomes on the course, are clearly revealing a sloppy decision-making process.

By all means, be perfectionistic about your preparation, be perfectionistic about your clubs, have them all checked for exact specifications that are perfectly suited to you. This is more of an exact science that you can and perhaps *should* be perfectionistic about. Be perfectionistic about your nutrition; make sure you take on fluid and fuel at regular and consistent times.

But do not be perfectionistic about when that ball and club meet each other. It is too delicate a relationship to support the weight of perfectionist ideals. In this respect it is not unlike a marriage; and maybe the fact we have all been given unrealistic expectations of the bliss marriage is supposed to bring us can be blamed for so many distressed and unhappy people.

To sum up: Be *perfectionistic* in the moments leading up to your swing. Be *realistic* in the moments after. If you have done the first part, then you have done your bit. Realise that and move on.

But just to finalise this section on perfectionism, the last word should come from someone who was not just one of the best golfers of all time, but who was also perceived to be a perfectionist, the legendary Ben Hogan. Hogan was portrayed as being a perfectionist but in his book *The Five Lessons,* he stated he became a great golfer when he learned to control his perfectionism. His quote sums it up perfectly: *No golfer can always be at the peak of his game; the key element is not to expect perfection but to expect mistakes.*

the mind factor

4 IGNORING CURRENT FORM

Once you have gathered your quality information on the lie, the distance, the pin position, the wind, the terrain, then you can make an informed choice of shot based on where your game currently is.

I will repeat that: W*here your game currently is.*

I recently heard one of the world's best golfers talk about his game in terms of A, B, C and D.

- His A game was obviously when everything was firing at 100%. He felt totally in control of his golf ball.
- His B game was still good but not at his peak.
- His C game was a bit of a struggle. A poor ball striking day.
- His D game was when he was *really* unaware of his game. A very poor ball striking day.

It was interesting to hear him say he had won tournaments with his C and his D game, but he said the key to those victories was in make decisions based on the level of his *current* game.

The popular Swede Jesper Parnevik put it slightly differently when he told *Golf World* magazine: "Here's the biggest difference between an amateur and a pro. On the range before the round, an amateur can slice 10 drives in a row – yet on the first tee he will still aim straight down the middle. For some reason, he still thinks he's going to hit the ball straight. If a pro slices three shots on the range, he will aim down the left on the first. If the amateur could only learn to work with what they have on the day, they would score a lot better than they do."

If you are out on the course and you are struggling with your D game, then make sure your decision-making reflects that in a conservative strategy. You will be amazed at how good it will feel to put a score together, when you are less than at your best.

5 PLAYING GOLF FOR OTHERS

Who do you actually play golf for? That may seem a stupid question. Your first answer will always be: "Myself, of course." Yet, have you ever given serious thought to this question? Do you *really* play golf for yourself? Or are there any other agenda when you step out on to the golf course?

Nobody, in my opinion, plays golf totally for themselves. As humans, we are simply hard-wired to seek approval from our peers. We like to fit in, we like to be appreciated and, above all, we like to feel worthy. Don't think you will ever totally free yourself of this. But let's take a closer look at what happens out on a golf course and some of the things people do.

I have noticed over the years there seems to be a few classic golfing personalities – and their characteristics, created from an often unconscious motivation to play the game for other people, do not aid their performance. You may well have played golf with one or more of them. Maybe you will even see something of yourself in with one or two of them – and if so, maybe you will decide to act differently.

MR EXHIBITION

Mr Exhibition has one really favourite club and one club he thinks is for sissies. Can you imagine what it is?

Mr Exhibition absolutely adores his driver. He reads all the latest articles on distance, he has the latest biggest-headed, shaft loaded tungsten whopper he can take out onto the course. He can't wait to show the others what he is capable of.

To Mr Exhibition, golf is about the adrenalin pump which comes from really flushing that drive miles down the middle, even if it means he has to send a couple of balls off the golf course. That is just part of the deal with being *The Man* off the tee.

To Mr Exhibition, the nonsense you have to carry out with the putter is for softies. What a waste of time. You can almost hear Mr Exhibition brag about how he three-putted after reaching the latest par 5 with a colossal drive and a 9-iron.

Mr Exhibition also usually wears bright or tight clothing and will nearly always have a needlessly gigantic golf bag.

MR BALL STRIKER

I have met so many of these people over the years, particularly out on the European Tour. They regard great ball-strikers with awe and reverence. They have a sneering disdain for those players who are not good ball-strikers – these inferior beings who just "chop it round". The fact they tend to chop it round in fewer shots than they do is of only minor importance, and glossed over. Mr Ball-striker is more concerned with hearing that particular strike, that special sound of club on ball that only they understand and appreciate… and that grants entry in to this most exclusive of clubs.

Woe betide anyone who has the audacity to score low or even win a tournament if they are not in the Ball-strikers" Club.

Mr Ball-striker usually wears dark clothing. He may well be lurking around in all black. He will more than likely have a set of blades in his bag. And he will lament the advent of hybrids, and give you chapter and verse on how adept he used to be with a 1-iron.

the mind factor

MR FRIENDS-AND-RELATIVES

Mr Friends-and-relatives is out there concerned. Very concerned.

He so much wants to do well because he knows he will get lots and lots of kudos from those around him – namely his friends and relatives.

The problem though for Mr F-and-R is, that he feels really bad when he has a poor score. He walks a tightrope of a certain score making him a good person and a certain score making him a bad person. He has blurred the boundary between what he *is* and what he *does*. Too much of his sense of self is housed on the direction his golf ball takes. That is far too much pressure for any human being to have on his or her shoulders. It is not, as esteemed golf coach Chuck Hogan once put it, "a "safe place" to play golf from". When we identify too much of our ego to any external situation, we become very vulnerable to the inevitable vagaries of results and outcomes.

Mr Friends-and-relatives is really quite a nice guy to play with. He is pretty courteous, doesn't wear anything too loud, he wants to blend in. You can see him getting very edgy on the course if play is slow or if he is playing badly himself. He just rushes around to "get out of the way". He doesn't stay for a drink in the bar after the game because he has "a lot on at the moment".

He is always the first person of your four ball at the club. Always.

MR BAD LUCK

Unfortunately, it will be your misfortune if you get to play with Mr Bad Luck because he is an absolute nightmare to play with.

Mr Bad Luck is always one piece of bad luck away from combustion. Yet, one of the curious things about Mr Bad Luck is that he will offer *you* the opportunity of having some good luck out on the course. As he shakes your hand on the first tee, with a firm clench of hands, he will inevitably serve up the phrase "Good luck today". But stand back you if you do get any, because you can bet *he* won't – and he'll certainly resent yours.

Or at least that is the way he sees it.

You can tell Mr Bad Luck a mile away. Hands on hips after the rest of the group has moved on, looking at the ground, shaking his head as that perfect 5-iron hits a hard part of the green and bounds through the back. Again! It can take just one good shot that doesn't turn out exactly as he thought it should to set him off. And, once he starts, the bad luck just seems to keep following him despite his obviously wonderful skill.

Professor Richard Wiseman has studied extensively the concept of luck over many years and, in a nutshell, his research suggests that luck is definitely out there but not in the way we conventionally think.

One of Wiseman's many experiments with luck involved setting up a shop with some money left on the doorstep. It showed that when "lucky" people walked into the shop, they tended to look down and find the money. What do unlucky people do? They just walk straight over it.

In other words, lucky people are lucky because they "think" that they are lucky. That leaves them open to and aware of opportunities for luck to come their way.

This is not to deny, of course, that some people have some terrible misfortunes in their life, which is clearly not their fault. What we are talking about is everyday run-of-the-mill luck you find out and about in life – and in particular, on the golf course. Mr Bad Luck never sees the ball that kicks away from the bunker or the ball that hits the trees and stays in bounds. He certainly doesn't see the full backswing he is afforded but has no right to expect when his ball runs into a copse. He doesn't see them because he is not looking.

the mind factor

As Jack Nicklaus said, "Golf is not meant to be fair." But if you go looking for your bad luck, you can always find it.

The real problem with Mr Bad Luck is that he has never grown up. Just like a child, he has an inflated sense of entitlement. He feels he should be luckier than he really is. This infantile sense of wanting the world to bend to his own wishes is the very thing that actually stops him from becoming the player he could possibly be.

Mr Bad Luck will always have a drink after the game but in the bar he is even more of a pain than out on the course, as his inability to look beyond his own paranoia makes him a bore.

MEET MR PROCESS

Joking aside, there is a serious element to this. If you notice yourself in one of the above, then you really are getting in your own way. All of this is easy to spot in others but somewhat more of challenge to fix in ourselves. Perhaps the most helpful thing we can do for our game is to commit to being Mr Process on the course.

Mr Process is very involved in what he or she *can* control. They play the game knowing the outcome can and will vary. On some days, they will go out onto the course and they will not score well. They will have some bad luck, some bad bounces, some poor breaks but this, they realise, is part of the nature of the game. In fact, it's the nature of life itself.

They focus very much on the process they need to follow on each and every shot they take. They have a principle that everything occurring *before* ball and club meet each other is 100% up to them but, as soon as ball and club meet each other, there is an element of uncertainty. They get very absorbed in the process and the challenge of each shot. As Tiger Woods said at his very best: "I get so lost in the *moment*, the challenge of hitting this shot, this task." It is as if this shot is the only thing that is occurring... and their attention is on it.

Just imagine how good it would feel to play golf like Mr Process. As part of his process, he also realises he is more than the direction of a golf ball. He himself is not too invested in outcome. If we can play the game and become absorbed in this task at hand, we can lose ourselves and create the possibility of entry into that special place called the zone. We get "lost in action".

That's a place where the mind actually wants to be. As human beings, we actually *crave* the opportunity to be so absorbed in something that we lose our sense of self. We *become the game* –and at that point, we are genuinely playing the game of golf.

It is possible to become so absorbed in an activity that really challenges mind and body. But to do so, we do need to be playing the game for ourselves, and not for others. Understand you will not achieve this all of the time; we are human with all of the faults and egotistical frailty that comes with the territory. But if we can begin to catch our self when we are playing the game for others and reasons other than golf, then we can bring our self back to the process.

That is something we can all aim at; and maybe it is the ultimate prize – to be able to sit back in the clubhouse after a game and reflect, regardless of the numerical outcome, we have done our bit that day. We have carried out our process on each and every shot. We have let the ball and the club meet each other and then we have dealt with the outcome and moved on to the next challenge. We can sit there and know we have *played golf.* We have played the game for the sake of the game – and that is more than enough reason for anybody.

CHAPTER 9

HOW TO SET EFFECTIVE GOALS

You might expect a chapter on goals to be at the start of this kind of book. However, I have deliberately left this section until now, as I think the whole area of goal-setting can be something of a minefield. Yet, if you can set the right goals for *you*, and then create an effective plan to turn those goals into physical action, they can be no less than the defining actions of your life.

Let me explain the potential problem with goal-setting. I have seen major winners who, having achieved their ultimate goal in golf, are almost crestfallen. Even as they are holding the trophy, a part of them is thinking: "Is that it?" In contrast, I have seen far too many talented golfers feeling under tremendous pressure because they are not where they feel they should be, based on some future goal-orientated structure. Because they are not where they should be, they then start to doubt themselves. They can even end up hating the very game they once loved.

Different as those scenarios are, we can pin both down to the type of goal-setting favoured by self-help books and literature around "life coaching". They will have you dreaming big and setting deliberately outrageous goals. I have come across dozens of golfers who have told me their goal is to be world number one.

To some degree this can be very effective, as it does at least give you a direction and it can light that internal fire which, for some, burns bright. But the problem I have found with creating deliberately outrageous goals is that they tend to become very *outcome-driven*, and lacking in the real and vital processes that help us achieve our goals.

Our decision to favour goals over processes has, I believe, been engendered by a conditioning that we always need to be "doing something to get somewhere". If we get good grades at school, then we can get into a good college. If we do well at college, then we can get into the "right" university. The right university will get us a job with "prospects", which can then give us the chance to build a solid career with terrific pension options. Then, when we draw our pension, we will finally be able to live our "dreams". Unfortunately, we die before it all falls into place!

Ok, it might well not be as dramatic as that; but you can see the direction I am moving here. I am *not* saying we shouldn't have big goals and big dreams. But I think it was John Lennon who said: "Life is what happens whilst we are busy making plans."

I am not in any way going to devalue goals here and I do think that a focused long-term *direction* is essential. But I do want you to consider shrinking the horizon on your goals to the much, much closer immediate future and mid-range future with a view to having a lot of what I call "little victories" on a daily basis. Over time, these add up to help you become the best golfer you can be. As tennis star Martina Navratilova famously said: "The moment of victory is so short that you *must* enjoy the journey."

It would seem the great football manager Sir Alex Ferguson enjoyed winning trophies; but I have it on good authority the thing he enjoyed the most is being at Manchester United's Carrington training ground early every morning, absorbing himself in the process of building and nurturing both players and teams. He was fascinated by the game of football, not just what the game of football would bring to him. His 25 years of success suggests there was something going on with him that many of the other clubs who hire and fire managers, just do not understand.

Just imagine if your ultimate goal or direction was to become the very best golfer you could possibly be. Would that focus you each day? Would that goal ever run out? Would it give you the freedom to just be and do? My guess is if you spent your life absorbed in

the mind factor

becoming the best player you could be and you had a real focus on improvement – but not at the expense of the love of the game – then you would still be able to *play* golf, as opposed to using golf for what golf might give you.

WHY YOUR BRAIN REJECTS GOAL-SETTING

The problem with many goals is we are just not wired correctly to carry out and complete the goals we set. We only need to witness what happens at the dawn of every New Year, when numerous people set wonderful goals for the "New Me". They are going to go on diets, they are going to get fit, and they are going to get a new job, they are going to change their life partner, they are going to travel more!

On and on it goes. It sounds wonderful; a few people even write out these goals. Yet, how many can look back halfway into the year and say they are on track with the goals they set earlier in the year? If you are one of those very rare individuals, then well done! You have overcome the basic wiring in your brain that, in fact, wants to keep you as you are and maintain the status quo.

I am not a neuro-scientist but as I understand it, the more "modern" part of our brain, our pre-frontal cortex, is the part of us that plans ahead, has great ideas, wants to conceptualise and, in general, lives more in a world of the future. Our older and more powerful unconscious mind has one primary function, and that is to *survive*. The way the unconscious tends to work is that if yesterday you did a series of behaviours which resulted in survival, then it would be a good idea to do more of the same today. For the unconscious, the status quo is good; the unknown future is absolutely terrifying.

There is no logic to this but it tends to make sense of things whereby people keep saying "I hate this job" when they discuss their occupation of 30 years. Or of people who say they hate the partner they are with but 20 years later are still in that abusive relationship. It may be a bad relationship but it is a *familiar* one. To step out of the status quo and into unfamiliar territory takes a massive effort and, for most people, it is just too easy to slip back into old patterns.

As I often warn people at seminars, when people hear the concept of Par 18 they love it; but probably fewer than 5% will do anything to act on the information because the pull of the familiar is so very strong. In many ways, to achieve your goals in life, I believe you need to have an understanding of the brain's innate desire to maintain what it has. You need tools and strategies that take this into account and allow you to move with a little stealth towards the things you value.

Sometimes, to be successful, you have to fly in the face of the intense discomfort the unfamiliar tends to promote. I want to present to you some ideas I have found useful on this theme; but also the very latest in research about what does and doesn't work when it comes to achieving your goals

INTENTIONS AND COMPLETIONS

There is a key process to achieving goals that I have seen work time and again. If you can really absorb yourself in some clear short term process-based goals – and you start to achieve these on a daily, weekly and monthly basis – then great things can happen. The strategy keeps your unconscious brain a little bit more calm and persistent. You start to become the kind of person who when they say they are going to do something, actually will do it. This can bring some real confidence. You take action that leads to momentum.

Just imagine for the next month when you get up in the morning, you write out in your journal three to five "actions" you are going to take today – actions that will be of benefit to your game and your on-going goal of becoming the very best player you can be. These points you write in your journal become your daily *intentions*. We have already spoken about the power of intention on the course itself, but the very same applies off the course, as well. Once you have written what you intend to do today, you set up the distinct probability you will follow through and turn your intention into a *completion*.

There is a big difference between thinking you are going to do something and saying you are going to do it. Even bigger is the difference between saying you are going to do something and actually writing it down. Writing is the physical part of thinking. Once you have your intentions set for the day, you will not want to get to the end of the day and see your intentions in your book that have not been completed. As a contrast, just how good it will feel to see those intentions become completions.

I truly believe that being successful by whatever definition you may have, is about compiling enough good days that begin to add up. When you have a consistent way of getting the best out of each day, you create a tremendous sense of momentum. You also get to have "little victories" each and every day, which feels good in and of itself. In effect, you are doing what Martina Navratilova suggested: you are becoming absorbed in the journey, not spending time fretting about the destination.

I have also found with this process that you start to think and plan your time much more efficiently. Instead of just saying you are going to work hard on your game, you are taking an active daily role in getting the best from your time. It is far too easy to just turn up at the range or the golf course and go through the motions as opposed to doing the things your game really needs.

SHAPE YOUR ENVIRONMENT

As we have discussed previously, your environment has a tremendous hold on your patterns and habits. The unconscious mind loves to maintain the status quo and a familiar environment will keep you running the same patterns. If you want to make some changes, then you need to understand how important it is to shape your environment to support your goals.

To give you a practical example, I have always known the practical benefits of having a training journal for the gym. To be able to record your sessions – weights you have used, intensity levels, any new personal best sessions – is vital to getting the best out of your time spent there.

I always had that bright shiny new training journal sat at home. The intention was to write in that journal after a session. Guess what generally would happen? I would go to the gym, do a good training session, then by the time I got back, other aspects of life had taken over. Calls needed to be answered, emails needed a reply, clients needed to be seen. My environment did not now support the filling in of my training diary. Despite me "knowing" and despite the intention, the goal wasn't achieved.

How did I work round that? Well, one thing I always do when I train is to take a quiet 10 minutes after a workout and sit with a drink. It feels good, it relaxes me and it is a reward for a good session. What is always with me? My gym bag. As obvious as it may sound, when I started to put the journal in my gym bag, the journal was filled in. The environment now worked for me as opposed to being against me.

I once heard a similar story of a guy who created what he called *The 30-Second Exercise Program*. He had trouble getting himself to keep fit and always found a way of avoiding doing the exercise he knew his body craved. He knew the environment was key and also the principle of getting started. So, what he did was "tell" himself

the mind factor

he was going to exercise for 30 seconds! He also made sure the first thing he did when he got out of bed was to put on his running shoes. That enabled him to get started with his program. Having started, he then exercised for much longer than 30 seconds. He would often run for an hour or go into his home gym. In effect, he had tricked his brain in a way that got both his job done and his goal achieved.

It may sound illogical but if you think about it, knowing what you need to do or want to do, and actually doing it, are two completely different things. That unconscious mind, which is programmed to keep things the same, needs to be outwitted in a way that supports your life. How can you apply this to your game? If you feel that Par 18 is important and you want to record your scores, then don't have the book at home; have it with you in your pocket. If you want to fill in your Intentions and Completions book, don't have that in your briefcase. Have it stationed by the toaster or your breakfast bar. Make the environment support your intentions.

MAKE YOUR COMMITMENT *ACTIVE*

Another sure-fire way to motivate yourself and follow through on your goals is to understand the difference between a commitment and an *active* commitment.

In an eye-opening recent study, social scientists Delia Cioffi and Randy Garner gathered together college student volunteers for an AIDS education project to be carried out at local schools. The researchers set up the study so the students were given one of two different sets of instructions.

○ Those who received *active* instructions were told if they wanted to volunteer, they should fill out a form stating they were willing to participate.

○ Those who received passive instructions were told if they wanted to volunteer, they should leave blank the form stating they were *not* willing to participate.

The research found the percentage of people who agreed to volunteer did not differ as a function of whether the instructions invited active or passive responding. They all said they would volunteer.

Yet, the astonishing difference was the percentage of people who actually showed up to participate in the project several days later. Of those who agreed to participate passively, only 17% actually appeared as promised: for those who agreed to participate actively (they filled in the form) a whopping 49% kept to their word and turned up to participate. In other words, of those who appeared, 74% were those who had *actively* agreed to participate for the programme!

A second way to make your commitment active is to *involve other people.* There is a big difference between me saying to myself that I am going to go to the gym tomorrow and actually saying to someone else that I am going to be at the gym. The former is a commitment; the latter is an active commitment.

Why are written or shared *active* commitments so much more successful at creating a behavioural change than those that are not? According to Robert Cialdini: "People make judgements about themselves based on observations of their own behaviour; they infer more about themselves based on their actions than on their non-actions."

If you want to get things done for yourself, write them down, or tell others you are going to do it. It creates a real issue in our brain if we don't then follow through. There is a cognitive dissonance we do not like.

A contrasting but no-less-effective strategy has been used by my colleague Tony Wrighton (**www.tonywrighton.com**). He works with the principle of loss aversion, whereby we would much rather avoid losing something than moving towards a potential gain. When

the mind factor

he agrees with his clients on a course of action, he makes sure they are fully on board and then he makes this wonderful, creative proposition to them. He asks them what charity or organisation would they under no circumstances ever donate money to. He then enters into a pact with them that if they don't act on his suggestion, they have to send a donation to their charity of "non-choice". It is a bit extreme, but nevertheless an effective means of getting people to take action.

A lot of this may sound negative. Let me balance that by declaring that we *can* get our brain to work for rather than against us.

As a rather surprising example, let us examine how Weight Watchers works. Science is actually offering an authoritative and surprisingly positive endorsement of the efficacy of Weight Watchers groups: two studies from the Medical Research Council, led by one of Britain's leading nutrition scientists, say that Weight Watchers really does work, and is a cheap and effective way for the NHS to tackle Britain's huge obesity problem.

The key strength of the Weight Watchers program appears to be in how it makes each participant accountable to other people – plus the sense of a shared goal with their immediate peers it promotes. Other people literally help you to lose weight.

This tells us something incredibly powerful – that no matter how much we will like to think of ourselves as strong-minded and individualistic, we are all massively influenced by the people who surround us. It is not an easy one to take on board, I know, but it is so important we become aware of how powerfully these subliminal messages from others have an impact on our behaviour.

The American motivational speaker Tony Robbins once said: "You will become by and large what your friends expect you to become." Much as I refuted that at the time and convinced myself it couldn't possibly have such a powerful effect, the results of the scientific studies above seem to confirm there is more than a grain of truth in his statement.

So what is going on with all of this?

I believe this is again the very strong evolutionary driver that we all have within us to fit in. If you think back to times gone by, it was absolutely essential you fitted in to the group with which you belonged. Indeed, go back a couple of hundred years and you didn't have the luxury of feeling the people you shared most of your time with were not "your type". You couldn't just up sticks and move to another country, or even county. You just didn't have those options. You had to fit in to survive. That was the deal you had. You had your community and that was pretty much that.

So, some pretty powerful evolutionary strings are still strongly pulling at us and the way we interact with the world. These evolutionary strings may well be out of date, but can still have a huge bearing on your success in the modern world.

FINDERS, MINDERS AND GRINDERS

So there we have a good number of key strategies to help you move towards your goals. They promote much better progress than those practised by "ideas people", those folk who you come across in your life, who are always full of information. They "know" all about the latest technology and techniques. Their talk is invariably in the future tense as they tell you what they are *going* to do. They usually have a book full of their great ideas… yet they never seem to make much progress in life. They never seem to get past the first base of the idea stage.

I remember a very wealthy and successful businessman tell me once that every successful business needed what he called Finders, Minders and Grinders. Finders, he explained, were the ones who sought out and found new things; the Minders were the ones who oversaw the production. But above all, he said, the real jewels in any

the mind factor

business crown were the Grinders. These are the people who actually got to work and made things happen. They were the action people, the implementers of the idea.

If you are on your own in pursuit of success, you need to be an amalgamation of all three… but you will really need to focus on the Grinder. You will need to take *action*, get things done. Have the willingness to fly in the face of your feelings of discomfort and to keep going until things get done. Overcome your brain and its natural tendency to want to keep the status quo.

All of those books that tell you to dream big and tap into the secret, tend to forget to mention how success is a result of being very focused on the here and now. It is fine to be clear about your future destination but you do need to be absorbed in the here and now, doing what you need to do *today*.

If you keep writing out your intentions and they become completions, on a daily basis, I guarantee you will create momentum; it will not be long before you are able to look back and realise the present you once had is a lot different the present you now have, and a lot more to your liking. All as a result of your consistent, process-based actions. You now have the tools, so get to work.

CHAPTER 10

FUEL FOR THE FIRE

In my opinion, an awful lot of books relating to the mind and how it affects your performance in golf, tend to miss one very important point. They talk endlessly about thinking the correct thoughts and taking charge of your emotions and/or reactions, which is fine; but if your brain is not being fuelled in a consistent and efficient way, then it is makes it almost impossible to put all that enlightened thinking into practice.

I have been fortunate to work with experts in the field of nutrition and hydration. I want to take this opportunity to share some of what I have found to be the most useful approaches, in terms of getting the best from your brain/body system.

THE MID-ROUND CRASH

In essence, the software (your mind) will only be as efficient as the computer that it is housed in (the brain). This may sound an arbitrary distinction: it is anything but. I became aware of the difference between the two when I started to get players to play the game "Super 6" which I mentioned in Chapter 8. Just to recap, Instead of looking at a golf course as 18 holes with two sets of 9 with all of the limitations it brings, Super 6 asks players to look at a round of golf as being six sets of three holes. The goal is simply to try to score as low as possible on each of the six sets of three holes. The beauty of the game is it shrinks the overall goal and allows you to play a little closer to the present moment.

I would get players to go away and do this for a minimum of 10 rounds of golf and then report back to me as to what patterns emerged within their "new" game. Overwhelmingly, the concept proved useful for most golfers as they began to understand where and how they tended to drop most of their shots. Some players would find a lot of shots would go adrift at the beginning of the round, showing a lack of effective preparation. Or they would finish badly again, perhaps showing how they had gone "forward" in time and been signing their scorecard on the 15th or 16th hole. Once they knew what the tendency was, they could at least shine the torch of awareness on to the problem and begin to do something about it.

Then, as I saw more and more of these scorecards come back to me, it began to strike me how there was a disproportionate amount of shots dropped around the 4th and the 5th set of three holes – holes 10-15. When I questioned players about this, they often said they were at a loss to understand why as they didn't feel they were nervous or they were angry or had done anything different. They often said they seemed to throw shots away for no reason at all.

The more I looked at it, the more I began to realise there *had* to be a link in a lot of cases to nutrition. After all, most golfers are out on the course for up to five hours, with little or no effective knowledge of how to hydrate and fuel their brain/body. Again, the more I looked and the more I asked them about their eating and drinking habits, the more it became obvious how a lot of poor shots, bad decisions and a lack of self-control could, and probably should be, explained by looking at the junk they continually put into their system. As much as a bacon and sausage sandwich may be a delight at the 9th – and as much as you may like to swig cola drinks or energy drinks – it can be safely said they are not the ideal option to support you in becoming the best golfer you can be.

I have also found in my own life that being aware of this element has made me realise just how bad my diet had become, even though I thought on the surface, I was eating reasonably healthy food. Dig a bit deeper and you do find some of the things that are sold to you

the mind factor

as being healthy are probably some of the worst things you can put into your body.

I am not in any way an expert in this field: I am only able to share with you what I personally have found to be useful. I emphasise these are only suggestions. But my main advice would be to become intensely curious about the food and the drink you put into your system. Explore differing ideas, but ultimately realise that your brain needs effective nutrition as much as your body; it can and will respond better for you if you at least give it half a chance by fuelling yourself correctly. Seek out the advice of experts in this field and you *will* notice a big difference in how you feel and, more importantly, how your brain responds to the demands you place on it during a round of golf.

Having said this, I will share with you one intervention in particular that has, for me, felt like a constant brain fog has been lifted.

WHEAT BELLY

One book I strongly advise you to take a look at is *Wheat Belly* by a cardiologist named William Davis MD. It opened my eyes to the potentially devastating effect wheat and wheat-based products can have on our brain/body system.

Wheat products elevate blood sugar levels more than virtually any other carbohydrate from beans to candy bars. This has very important implications for body weight, since glucose is unavoidably accompanied by insulin. The higher the blood glucose after consumption of food, the greater the insulin level. The more fat is deposited. This is why eating a three-egg omelette – which triggers no increase in glucose – does not add to body fat, while two slices of whole wheat bread increases blood glucose to high levels, triggering insulin and growth of fat – particularly abdominal or deep visceral fat.

It is not just the weight gain you need concern yourself with; this can also affect your brain in terms of loss of concentration and poor decision-making. Things which directly lead to dropped shots. This is because your brain is highly sensitive to the wide variety of substances that gain entry to the blood, some of which can provide undesirable effects should they cross into your amygdala, hippocampus, cerebral cortex and other brain structures. In this instance, wheat can cause your brain to go haywire. My suggestion would be to eliminate bread from your diet.

HOW TO FEED
YOUR BRAIN

Phil Richards (**www.philrichards.com**) is one of the foremost experts in this field. Phil has been a consultant to numerous athletes from across many sports and I strongly recommend you check out his work. I am grateful for his help and his compilation of the following eight tips for maximising brain function with effective nutrition. Phil writes:

You have been entrusted with the care and feeding of the most extraordinary and complex creation in the universe. Your brain is a maze of trillions of connections capable of performing 20 million calculations per second. It has three major components:

Neurons: brain cells that power the communication message.

- Neurotransmitters: chemicals that create the message.
- Receptors: proteins that receive the message.

Home to your mind and personality, your brain houses your cherished memories and future hopes. It gives you purpose and passion to live life to the full and achieve your dreams. But what do you feed your brain for it to function optimally?

1, We are beginning to learn that if you want a brain that functions to its full potential and provides a lifetime of vital service, you must pay close attention to dietary fat. Nothing you put in your mouth is as agreeable or disagreeable to the intricate structures of your brain cells as fat. Your brain is the body's fattiest organ – 60% of the dry weight of the brain is made up of various fat-like substances.

2. The chemistry of that fat can profoundly influence the very architecture of your brain cells, the profusion or scarcity of all-important dendrites and synapses, the linchpins of intelligence, learning, memory, attention, concentration and mood. Omega 3 fish oil, more precisely the part called DHA (docosahexaenoic acid) is the building material for synaptic communication centres. You can't create more synapses, dendrites, or receptors that increase your brain's potential without a robust supply of DHA so you better make sure you have it in abundance in your diet or your brain will suffer.

3, Like a growing tree, any time a nerve cell makes a new branch it requires new raw materials. Without adequate DHA available, branching out cannot happen. If brain fats are not available in needed amounts you will not grow new dendrites & axons and have a very hard time learning new material. A single neuron may make up to 40,000 connections with other cells, and you have approximately 100 billion neurons in your brain. The place where these cells connect is the synapse. The portion of the nerve making the connections is called the synaptic membrane. This part of the nerve has the highest concentration of DHA than almost any other tissue in the body. If DHA is in abundance, communication within the brain is carried out very efficiently and you have mental clarity; however, if there are deficient DHA levels due to poor dietary habits then communication becomes inefficient and you have brain fog. So eat your fatty fish – sardines, mackerel, wild salmon – or supplement with pharmaceutical grade fish oil to ensure you have good brain health.

4. The language our brain uses to direct our mood is determined by "words" called neurotransmitters. Neurotransmitters are the runners that race to and from the brain, telling every organ inside of us what to do. Neurotransmitters touch the life of every cell. Neurotransmitters affect mood, sleep, concentration, weight, and can cause adverse symptoms when they are out of balance.

5. Living at your peak – when every day is a good day at work, when enjoyment comes easily, when you feel strong and healthy – can be directly traced to a balanced brain. This occurs when all four of your primary bio-chemicals (Dopamine, Acetylcholine, GABA, and Serotonin) are transmitting properly and in the right proportions. Each of your neurotransmitters is essential to proper brain health;

when any one of them is deficient or out of balance with the others, problems result which can ultimately affect all body systems, leading to very serious mental health conditions.

6. There are four types of attention disorders that relate to the four neurotransmitters. Inconsistent attention indicates a deficiency of dopamine, whereas if we are careless and have trouble misplacing things, acetylcholine deficiency is indicated. A lack of attention and impulsive actions are a product of insufficient GABA. If we are low in serotonin we will lose our ability to grasp concepts quickly.

7. Neurotransmitter levels can be depleted many ways. Stress, poor diet, neurotoxins, genetic predisposition, drugs (prescription and recreational), alcohol and caffeine usage can throw these levels out of optimal range. The good news is that we derive these neurotransmitters again from our diet primarily from quality protein sources – apart from Acetylcholine which can be derived from such foods as almonds, blueberries, cabbage & cauliflower.

8. Your brain is the most complex, mind-blowing organ in the universe. It weighs only about three pounds, usually around two per cent of the body's weight. Unbelievably it is 80% water. The brain uses 25% of the oxygen we breathe and up to 70% of the glucose we consume when at rest. So make sure you keep well hydrated, get some exercise to keep oxygen and blood flow to the brain, and

eat good carbohydrates like fruits & vegetables
to keep a constant supply of glucose to the brain.
Understanding what you eat will have a significant
effect on how well your brain functions. Remember!
You are your brain.

THE IMPORTANCE OF WATER

Water makes up about the same percentage of our bodies as it does the planet – approximately 70%. Since our bodies are continually using and losing water, a conscious effort to maintain hydration by replacing lost water is vitally important.

Because water is needed for virtually every biological process, chemical reaction and mechanical action that takes place in our body, it is crucial to mental and physical performance. As a major component of the blood, water is the delivery system that gets oxygen to each cell of the body. Within the lymphatic system, water carries away waste products as well.

It ionizes salts, producing the electrolytes necessary for electrical activity across the cell membranes. It enables us to move our joints and digest our food. Water is essential for the proper use of protein in the body and for the development of the nerve network during learning.

Most people wait until they are thirsty before drinking water but thirst lags *way* behind the body's water needs. If for instance you carry out an exercise program and you rely solely on thirst to remind you to replenish water, it may take your body a full 24 hours after each workout to return to proper hydration levels. Even as you sit and read this page, your body is maintaining a constant, light perspiration, and stress or more strenuous activities increase the amount of perspiration lost.

You even lose water (in the form of vapour) every time you exhale!

On a typical day, two-and-a-half to three quarts of water are lost by your body. You can see why we all need to take frequent sips of good-quality water throughout the course of each day. There is surely no simpler, more natural way to both feel better and function better.

This book is about learning to think more efficiently and to be able to direct your attention to the areas of your game and your life that are useful. As I mentioned at the start of this chapter, this is almost impossible to do if you are not looking after your brain with good nutrition and hydration.

When playing the game Super 6, aim to drink some water after each set of three holes and take on some food/fuel like blueberries or nuts after every two sets of three holes. Commit to doing this for the minimum of 10 rounds and just notice what that does to your golfing experience. Do not be surprised to find you feel better when you play golf.

And, if you do, might it be a good idea to look at your general nutritional health in other areas of your life? Only a suggestion, but one I know you will look back on as being one of the best decisions you have ever made.

CHAPTER 11

COACHING IN GOLF – AND OTHER SPORTS

Although this book's purpose is to show you how different thinking can lead to better and more enjoyable golf, I hope this doesn't imply any rejection of technical coaching. I believe 100% in swing technique, and coaching. To work with a great coach is to embrace the possibility of fulfilling your true potential. Great coaching is an opportunity to shorten the learning curve and when it is done well, it is a terrific partnership. For the good of your game and also the good of your business or your life, it will pay dividends if you invest in good coaching.

These days, you have the opportunity to take advantage of the fact that PGA professionals are highly trained. To even become a professional takes a good three years of dedicated work learning about the art of coaching. Then, once qualified, most of the better coaches will have embarked on a series of professional development courses to improve their skills and understanding of the various facets of the game of golf.

For many years, I was personally involved in the PGA's Continuing Professional Development courses driven by their energetic and visionary head of training Dr Kyle Philpotts. Up to that point, around the turn of the millennium, most golf coaches did little or no further training once they had qualified with the PGA. That has all changed now for the better and it gives you the opportunity to take advantage of this learning and development.

That said, I do want you to pick your coach carefully or, if you already have a coach and you are thinking about a change, I want you to really *take ownership* of the learning process. Your coaching really must be tailored to you as an individual, as opposed to being pressganged into a certain "method" of learning the game. I have been involved in golf a long time now and I have seen many methods come and go. My observation would be that any method will suit certain people at certain times of their golfing lives, depending on what they currently do with the club. The problem arises when all players are trying to fit in with a certain vision of a method coach.

Ultimately, what really matters, is how you deliver that clubface into the ball and on what path the club is traveling. This is something the great John Jacobs has been telling us for the best part of 60 years. The ball doesn't care what method you use, but it does care what the club is doing at impact. A repeating swing is a good swing because it can control the flight of the golf ball.

I have seen many careers ruined because a player has felt the need to "go to the next level'... and the next level only seems to be attainable by changing your swing mechanics. I'm not convinced that's the case. The beauty of utilising the concept of The Three Phases of Golf is that it helps you get more – get the best – out of your current swing. It aims to give you the tools to get out onto the golf course and work with what you have.

I am not saying you shouldn't try to improve your mechanics. But good mechanics will only get you so far and, if you don't look at and work on The Three Phases of Golf, you will always court being that "great practice ground golfer" I have seen far too many times over the years.

One thing I would urge you to discuss with your coach is how much attention he or she pays to the mental part of the game. Does he consider it an important part of your work together?

I would also ask you to discuss with your coach, how much time he will take to be out on the course with you. Most football coaches will watch their players on a football pitch; most tennis coaches will watch their players play matches on a tennis court. Yet, a huge number of golf coaches will never see their players hit a single shot on a golf course! This is madness because I absolutely guarantee what

the mind factor

you do on a course and what you do on the range, may well be totally different. Remember our old friend context again. You will behave differently depending on the context you are in; and as we have said over and over again in this book, the context of the range and the context of the golf course environment are two very different places.

Make sure your Pro gets you out onto the course and plays a few holes with you at the very least. In an ideal world, he should see you play in a competition and see how things stand up under pressure. He should be checking all of your Three Phases of Golf in the environment of competition.

If you have any doubt about this or maybe you want to get a second opinion on your mental game, then it would be worth looking at the **MIND FACTOR** website **www.themindfactor.com** to locate your nearest **MIND FACTOR** coach.

WHAT YOU CAN LEARN
FROM OTHER SPORTS

If I think back to my own career in coaching, I think some of my most rewarding moments and greatest opportunities to learn have been when I have looked outside my own golfing box and had the chance to learn from coaches and players in other sports. Here are seven whose insights have helped shape and develop my own ideas on improving performance:

AMERICAN FOOTBALL: LOU HOLTZ

I remember being on the range with Graeme McDowell at Lake Nona and being introduced to the legendary American Football coach Lou Holtz. Now in his late 70s, Holtz had one of the most outstanding college football coaching careers in the history of the game. Coach Holtz was working hard on his golf game when I met him but he quickly began to talk about some of his own coaching philosophies that can be applied to almost anything. He said he felt the most important concept he had used in his career was the concept of **WIN**. When he mentioned this, the little voice inside my head was having its usual rant about "the bleedin" obvious' until Holtz went on to explain that **WIN** was an acronym for What's Important Now?

He said so many times teams will be focused on what happened last week or what may happen at the end of the season; but all he kept drilling into his players was to focus on the task right in front of them. What's important now? The tackle which needed to be made, the pass, the play or the interception. The simplicity of the message was so profound but so vitally important. Coach Holtz understood the concept of Attention and he knew that a player's attention was either on something useful or not useful. **WIN** kept his players" attention on the here and now, the task at hand.

RUGBY LEAGUE:
NATHAN BROWN AND PAUL ANDERSON

I have also been fortunate to do some work in Rugby League and had the chance to spend time with two great coaches – Nathan Brown of St Helens and Paul Anderson of the Huddersfield Giants. In the world of Rugby League, you very quickly learn that mental toughness is not optional; it is a pre-requisite to stay involved in the game. It may well be one of the toughest of all sports because for 80 minutes the players just simply go at each other at full speed with little or no body protection.

The learning I gained from these two great coaches was that even though Rugby League is a team sport, a team operates at its maximum when each player has a *very clear focus* on what he needs to do in the game. He has a couple of key jobs to do and if he focuses on his role, everything else will take care of itself.

The teamwork ethic works beautifully when a bunch of individuals are very clear about what they need to do. The problem arises when a player strays away from his role and his attention is diluted, worrying about aspects of the game that really are of no concern to him.

One of the wonderful tools these coaches use to deal with this, is to have the players simply write out on a sheet of paper placed above their shirt in the dressing room, the two or three jobs they are going to do on the pitch. Once they have written down their jobs, the mind is then "programmed" to carry out that task. They have also made a commitment to themselves and, more importantly, a commitment to their team mates (active commitment). Writing out what you are going to focus on during the game doesn't mean you are guaranteed to do it but, in my experience, it massively increases your chances.

TEST CRICKET: MICHAEL VAUGHAN

My two greatest sporting passions have always been golf and cricket. If I were to be pushed into a corner and forced to pick, I would have to say that of the two, I would sooner watch cricket than golf. The closest thing to heaven for me would probably be sitting in the grandstand at Lords on the first day of an England Test match. So you can imagine how I felt to have the opportunity to work with the then England captain Michael Vaughan in the summer of 2005 in what turned out to be, as many observers have said, the greatest Test Series of all.

England managed to wrestle the Ashes back from the Australians after the best part of 20 years being ritually humiliated by the old enemy. It may have started with previous captain Nasser Hussain, but Vaughan created a totally new culture within the England set-up. He had taken the team from being perennial losers and molded them into a formidable unit.

It became very clear to me that Vaughan had freed the players up to go out and express themselves on the cricket pitch, as opposed to being scared of making mistakes. His core philosophy was to go out and express yourself but, above all, to *enjoy* your cricket. As obvious as that sounds, I think we spend far too much of our life striving to be somewhere other than where we are at the moment. We are always doing something to get somewhere else. Vaughan reminded his players to embrace these golden moments that were actually happening right here and now.

Vaughan always believed enjoying your cricket was a decision you made which didn't have to be dependent on the score of the game. It can be argued in terms of a chicken-and-egg situation that you are bound to enjoy your cricket more if you are winning. But, by the same measure, there is a proven correlation between becoming more successful and starting to win *as a result of* deciding to enjoy yourself.

As we have said already in this book, if you wait for the golf ball to fly exactly where you want it to, then you are probably going to be in for a long wait. Yet, when you decide to enjoy the process, in spite of what the ball may or may not be doing, then you set yourself free to enjoy the game. You will probably be pleasantly surprised as to what a better attitude overall can do for the details of your game.

TEAM SKY: SIR DAVE BRAILSFORD

I have never met Bradley Wiggins but, like everyone, I was phenomenally impressed by his performance in becoming the first Brit to win the Tour de France and then following it up by winning

Olympic gold only a matter of days after riding triumphantly up the Champs Elysees.

Of course, Wiggins deserves massive credit for the guts and determination with which he has overcome his own personal battles in the bid to become the best he can at his sport. What is clear, though, is that Wiggins has been fortunate to have a brilliant coaching team around him. Led by performance director Dave Brailsford at Team Sky, Wiggins has often commented on how much his coaching has been part of his development.

Brailsford has a mantra that has become something of a buzz-word or phrase in almost all coaching circles. "The aggregation of marginal gains" is now entrenched as a concept in the mind of most people who are interested in elite performance. Aggregation of marginal gains is, in its simplest form, a culmination of a lot of seemingly minor things that, put together, all add up to peak performance. For Brailsford, it is a labour of love to look at the smallest of details, to see if it could possibly add something to the team effort. From looking at the kind of pillows his team sleeps on to the shape of the helmets they wear on the cycle, they know at Team Sky they are not going to be beaten as a result of poor preparation.

They are the ultimate example of a group of people who look at Phase One and do *everything in their power* to make sure they are ready when the race starts and to be free to give their all. Phase Two may present some curve balls – the tyres may get punctured, protestors may jump out, the weather may be horrific, all of these things they cannot control – but they know all the things they can control have been attended to.

In your own game, you almost certainly don't have the time to go into the level of intricate detail that Team Sky do. But you can look at your game with a mindset of 1%. What aspects of your current attitude and preparation could be improved by a 1% that, if added up, could make a difference to your score?

It may seem insignificant but what kind of music do you play in the car before you play golf? Is it music that puts you in the right state of mind to be at your best? What kinds of food do you eat? Do you have a coffee before you play? Do you spend time on your mobile? The research is suggesting this could be a very bad thing for your brain. What is the first thing you do to warm up? What kind of fuel do you carry in your bag?

I am sure you get the idea. All of these seemingly unimportant details could have an impact on your score. Not for one minute am I saying that making sure you listen to relaxing music will stop a bad swing from producing poor shots. But, I know from experience, one of the greatest boosters of confidence, is knowing you have looked at your game in detail and you are ready to play. You are prepared.

You may not go into the detail Dave Brailsford does, but I strongly recommend you sit down with a piece of paper and consider some areas of your game you haven't looked at before which just might make a 1% difference. If you play the game at the highest level and you intend to make a career out of this, I would say this exercise is an absolute must.

FOOTBALL: SIR ALEX FERGUSON

I believe that even if I wasn't a Manchester United fan (yes, I know that we were all getting along really well up to this point!), I would still have a tremendous admiration for what Sir Alex Ferguson has done over the years in becoming one of the most successful football managers of all time.

I once had the opportunity to present some ideas to the first team at their Carrington training ground. With Sir Alex sitting right on the front row with a pen and a notebook in hand, it may well have been the most daunting presentation I have ever had to do!

the mind factor

I had done Phase One pretty well, though, in the sense I knew my material; and as I stood up to see a sea of heroes, faces including superstars such as Ryan Giggs and Paul Scholes, I did manage to "let go" and let the training take over.

I talked to the team about the importance of decisions and how a decision made now, in terms of your actions, may not seem to be of great importance today, but could have a huge influence way down the line. A decision to eat better will not change much today but the same decision adhered to for a number of weeks, months and then years could be profound. The healthy body and mind would begin with a decision.

I made the point that one of the reasons Sir Alex had been so successful was the fact that he had been prepared to make some very tough decisions over the years. He must have had numerous occasions when the easy way out was to avoid making a decision about a player who, to all others, may have been a hero at the club. Yet he made decisions, very tough decisions about legendary players such as David Beckham and Roy Keane, who had given the club their best years but who, he knew, needed to be moved on. These tough decisions have been one of the pivotal factors in managing one of the biggest clubs in the world for an astounding 25 years. He could have just gone with the flow but something inside him must have known that the decisions, as tough as they were, *had* to be made.

You may well have to make some tough decisions in your own life. You may have to decide for the good of your game that certain people you spend time with are just not supporting you with your goals. You may need to make a big decision about where you play or the management company you are going to sign for. You will have decisions you can shy away from… or you can fight the feelings of discomfort that you will have and resolve to make the decision you know is important for your future.

The more uncomfortable a decision seems to be, the more important it probably is. Maybe some football managers who didn't make the tough decisions they should have made, now look back on their career with a touch of sadness. Like him or loathe him, as Sir Alex looks back on his career, you can be sure he must know his success has been laid on the foundation of the courage to make tough decisions.

AMERICAN FOOTBALL: BILL WALSH

The title of a book by another great coach, Bill Walsh of the San Francisco 49ers – *The Score Takes Care of Itself* – pretty much sums up my own philosophy on getting results and has, hopefully, been reflected in the direction this book has taken.

So often, when we get obsessed by outcomes over which we have no control, we get in our own way. Tension is created by a mind that is sitting too far into the future and is also hampered by what has happened in the past. To be absorbed in your process is to be absorbed in an area you *can* control. You have the right to put 100% effort into whatever you choose to direct your attention to. You do not have the right to believe the outcome will be exactly as you want it to be. The more you are focused on *your* process and what *you* can do, the more successful you will be.

The by-product also is that I would almost guarantee you will be happier on a day-to-day basis as you enjoy the journey of what you are doing, as opposed to stressing over the final destination. *The Score Will Take Care of Itself* is a representation of Three Phases Of Golf thinking. You do what you can in Phase One with as much detail to attention and focus as you may require; you then let go and become involved in the action, while knowing you will deal with the outcome. Simply because you have done all you can in Phase One.

Of course results matter. Most of us are in a "results business" in one way or another. But I have never found that focusing too much on results does anything other than create stress and limit capability. You allow results to come through having your attention in the right place and a perspective that is liberating as opposed to restrictive.

I hope you have enjoyed this chapter as a way to encourage you to look at other disciplines and other sports to broaden your view. Look through the lens of not knowing, as opposed to knowing it all. We tend to get bogged down in what we do by the pervasive idea we don't do it that way in golf because we have always done it this way. If you begin to look at things with an open mindset, you can then break free of the shackles of dogma and determinism.

As Richard Bandler, the Co-Founder of NLP, once said, "In all fact, there is a little fiction and in all fiction, there is a little fact." Have a look outside your current world, take in the opinions of others, be open enough to believe there may be a better way. But, above all, understand we are meant to enjoy the journey as well as the destination. Golf is a great laboratory to test things out and learn about yourself in the meantime. Make sure you take that opportunity with both hands.

CHAPTER 12

THE THREE PHASES IN YOUR LIFE

There is a definite link between the mind set you need to perform at your best on a golf course, and the approach needed to bring success to other areas of your life. Because of this, I am often asked to do talks for business leaders, teams and sales people.

The more I have worked in this area, the more I am seeing how the way you prepare, execute and respond to a golf shot, is reflected in almost everything you do. As you do in one, you will tend to do in all to a certain degree.

Already during the pages of this book, we have looked at the fact that on every shot you play, two of the Three Phases are completely under your control and one isn't. Yet, that Phase which is least under your control gets the most attention and is the focus of almost all the standard world of instruction. Both inside and outside of golf, many of the issues and problems we have are because we try to control Phase Two.

To recap, the secret here is to do all you can in Phase One to prepare, and then *let go* in Phase Two; knowing you have the capability and the determination to deal with whatever the outcome is in Phase Three. Here, we will look at how we could apply this principle in various non-golfing environments.

 SALES

PHASE ONE: BEFORE THE MEETING

Set a very clear *intention* of what you want to achieve. Do the necessary background work on your client and his company, his needs and wants. Try to engineer the environment you are going to meet in as much as possible. Try to meet your client away from their normal location. Aim to sit with them one-to-one in their favourite restaurant. Have all of the details he may need from you planned out in your head. Go through the possible objections and potential pitfalls of what you are going to propose to him. In effect, do all you can *before* you meet.

PHASE TWO: DURING THE MEETING

Make a firm commitment to just let go. Allow yourself to be in the here and now, focusing on your client and the conversation you are having. You have set your onboard computer prior to the meeting: now, it is just a case of being with him and reacting to what he presents to you in this unique moment in time. Expect neither to make the sale nor miss the sale. You are operating from the freedom of a "let's see what happens" mind set. You are free to let yourself come out, as opposed to being some kind of contrived "sales" individual. Allow yourself to interact with the environment and the conversation that emerges.

PHASE THREE: AFTER THE MEETING

Make a firm commitment before any of this interaction that you will deal with the outcome of the meeting. If it is good and he buys into you, well that is fine. If he doesn't, process the meeting in a way that means you will *not* get emotionally attached to the outcome. Commit to feeling that, whatever happens, you will move on to the next call, the next situation, the next meeting. You are safe in the knowledge this meeting is a reflection of something you *do* as opposed to something that you *are*.

the mind factor

Can you see the freedom in this approach? All you have to do is accept the fact that Phase Two is not under our control. Your client may be in the middle of a divorce; his kids may be playing up; he just might not have any money. There are a whole bunch of things that could happen in Phase Two that you have absolutely no control over. Yet, so many people in business tie themselves in knots and stress about the outcome, which is not under their control.

Can you imagine the freedom of 100% committing that you will deal with any outcome? If you are not afraid to fail, then you might just find you are not afraid to achieve. We weren't taught this in school – in fact most of us were taught the opposite – but it is at the heart of mental toughness.

2 PRESENTATIONS AND SPEECHES

PHASE ONE: BEFORE THE PRESENTATION

You can't guarantee a presentation will go well if you do your preparation well beforehand – but you can pretty much guarantee it will go badly if you don't. Over the years, I have made a rule that you always need to assume things will go wrong with the people hosting the event. The projector will break down, the seats won't be set as you want them to be, there will be noise coming from another room. Some of this is unavoidable; but what you can do is get there early, have your own projector, and make sure you have a flip chart. You can make sure you have written out the key points of your presentation. You can research the audience to ensure you know what they are likely to want. You can have your videos ready to play, your hand-outs printed, your PowerPoint presentation memorised. All of these factors you can influence. You still have the ability to prepare as well as you possibly can.

PHASE TWO: DURING THE PRESENTATION

Again, once you start, you can have a clear intention of what you are trying to say, but audiences are like individuals. One day you can say something and the audience thinks it's the funniest thing they have ever heard; the next night you say exactly the same thing at the same time and you look out at a sea of blank faces. You only need a couple of people in the room who are hell bent on proving they know more than you and you are in for a challenging evening.

Just as we have discussed with a golf shot, you cannot control an audience. You can influence them just as you can influence a golf ball but you cannot totally control how people are going to react. The best presentation occurs spontaneously when you have done your prep and you then just let go and allow yourself to interact with the people sat in front of you. The feeling of letting go is not dissimilar to how you feel when you just let your body take over on a golf shot. There is a freedom in not trying to control the outcome.

PHASE THREE: AFTER THE PRESENTATION

One of the most important lessons I learnt myself with this was the understanding that if you have 50 people sat in an audience, then you will have 50 individual people with totally differing experiences of the same talk. Each person is hearing your words and watching your actions from inside his or her own unique filter on the world. That very filter is influenced by all of their life experiences to this

the mind factor

point and, subconsciously, they are having an experience that is in a way contaminated by their own past experiences. When you stand up and begin to speak, you might look and sound uncannily like one of their most hated teachers. They may well not be aware of this themselves, but you can bet some feeling of distrust towards you will be firing in their brain. They may not know why they don't really like you, but it will be going on.

They may, on the other hand, have a cascade of pleasant feelings as your words and actions trigger some really positive emotions from their past history. You cannot control this; but again, you can control your reaction to it.

3 RELATIONSHIPS

Again, we get ourselves in such a tangle in life because we expect people to behave in a certain way. We think that because we have done certain things for them, then they should do certain things for us. That is Phase Two thinking. We are again attempting to make certain of something that will always be unpredictable. Human beings are not unlike that golf ball in the sense we can do a lot of things to influence them, but ultimately, we cannot control another human being. Effective Three Phase thinking would or should look a bit like this:

PHASE ONE: RAISING AN "ISSUE"

Decide what you want to say to the other person. It may be what they want to hear or it may not; the only thing you can do is present, as honestly as possible, what you think and feel. You are letting them know what their behaviour is doing to you. You are not stating what they do is right or it is wrong, you are just letting them know how their actions are affecting you. In effect, you are deciding to paint as clear a picture for them of your perspective as possible. That said, when you have done that, you need to understand that Phase Two is again out of your control.

PHASE TWO: THE REACTION

You have presented your side of the story. You have filled in the details of the picture for them. Now here is the tricky bit. As much as you are certain of your case being the correct one, we are into the golden rule that a Phase Two situation is *not* under your control. You cannot make someone react in the way you want them to react. "Why doesn't (s)he understand my feelings?" This is one of the most futile of human remarks. He or she is representing your words and your actions in their *own* map of the world. Again, to stress the point, this representation is out of your control. You have done the best you can to influence it but you cannot control it.

PHASE THREE: YOUR RESPONSE

So they react to what you have said. They act in a certain way that, in the past, would have really upset you. But because you have ingrained the concept of the Three Phases into your heart and soul, you realise you have done all you can in Phase One. Phase Two has happened but now in Phase Three, you decide you are going to take charge of how you respond to the situation. Just because someone doesn't agree with you or see your point of view or your idea, it

the mind factor

doesn't mean you have to react by being angry or upset, just like the shot that pulled up short of the green or the putt that hit the spike mark. You recognise what is in and out of your control. You begin to master your world by focusing on being as efficient and precise as possible in Phase One, you let go in Phase Two and you deal with the outcome in Phase Three.

As you can see with all of these examples, the principle is simple and consistent and the formula is one that I believe you can use efficiently in so many areas of your life.

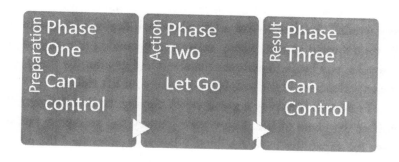

It takes discipline and determination to prepare well for Phase One. It takes the courage to assemble all of the necessary details, put your attention in the right place and then get yourself ready to let go in Phase Two and just let the situation play out. Once there has been a result, you then in Phase Three make a lifelong commitment to deal with the outcome of the golf shot, the business deal, the exam, the relationship or whatever situation in life is presented to you. With this mind set, you become very tenacious and the sort of person who gets things done.

I think that in the modern world, we have become so scared of the results in Phase Two that we don't attend to what we need to do in Phase One and then wonder why the world is not bending to our whims and desires. There has been far too much written about "believing", that you just have to ask the universe for what you want; but back in the real world we are going to hit the shot off-line, people will reject us, we won't get the job. But that does not mean we can't bounce back and respond in a way that enables us to keep moving toward the future we desire.

In so many ways, golf is a terrific example of this because even the very best hit an awful lot of bad shots. The very best don't win even *most* of the time. It is a game of imperfection in a world that craves certainty. Yet, the more you embrace these very simple principles, you start to live a life of *possible*. Remember another of our key words? You start to live a life where you deal with the setbacks that are thrown at you, where, instead of becoming scared of more setbacks, you begin to embrace the chaos and go after the situations, the experiences and the people who make your life richer.

To do that is to play a game worth playing, be that the game of golf or the game of life. Enjoy your journey and recognise you do have the capability to be resilient. When you understand the power of focused attention, you may not achieve everything in life that some of the books promise, but you *will* achieve an awful lot.

CONCLUSIONS

I hope you have enjoyed our journey together through The Three Phases of Golf and the **MIND FACTOR** as applied to your game and, perhaps, even some areas of your life.

As I said at the beginning of the book, it has been a long journey for me as a player and a coach. None of what I have said is meant to be taken as some kind of gospel. It is a collection of ideas I have found to be useful with a great number of players, no more and no less. What I would ask you to do, having read this book, is to think how you might apply some of the ideas to yourself or your clients but in a way that is personal to you. I have failed if you just take my ideas literally and copy them.

Ultimately, these ideas are offered as tools to create a mind set that is open to *possibility*. For too long, the game of golf has suffered as a result of too many "experts" saying it has to be done this way or that. For me, the individual is sacred and you have to find your way to play the game in a fashion that enriches your life and gives you pleasure along the way, not just as a means to "get somewhere". The question of why you play golf is for you to ponder but it needs to be *your* answer, as opposed to somebody else's conditioning.

Golf presents a wonderful opportunity to be involved in a game that mirrors so much of what goes on in life. There is a part of golf we can control (Phase One); there is a part we need to let go of and merge with, knowing the outcome will be unpredictable most of the time (Phase Two); and we then need to make a commitment to being able to deal with whatever that little white sphere does (Phase Three). As this chapter suggests, this is surely a reflection of so much in the rest of our life.

As we have said over and over in this book, if you are prepared to deal with the outcome of Phase Two, then you get to play a game

WITHOUT fear. This is where real consistency comes from; not in the mistaken belief we can perfect the swing (because we can't), but in the understanding that we *can* deal with unfavourable outcomes. The better we get at that, the more freedom we have to be absorbed in the joy of Phase One and the opportunity to create a golf shot here and now in this unique moment in time. If we keep doing that, we become a tough customer to beat.

This also applies in other areas of our life. The less fear we have of an outcome because we have prepared ourselves to deal with disappointment, the more we take on the opportunities that life can offer us. In many ways, we go from being childish, where we stamp our little feet if the world is not yielding to our own personal whim and fancy, to becoming child*like* again, in the sense we are not afraid to seek out and explore possibilities.

Play more games of golf where you are playing just for the sake of being here and now, out on the course *today*. Not as a means to get your handicap down or to get on tour or win more money, but as a means to enjoy what you have in front of you – as opposed to some far-off perception of what a future may or may not bring.

In the same way, in your life, realise the opportunities you have and the need to develop a steely sense of certainty that you are capable of dealing with the dropped shots, tops and shanks that life *will* throw at you. As you do this, don't be surprised to find there will be a few birdies along the way.

And when they come along, don't be afraid to let a smile creep onto your face, in the knowledge you are living your life as opposed to thinking about your life. There is a world of difference; and I hope in the short time we have had together, I have been able to at least ask you some good questions – even if I haven't supplied you with all of the answers.

Enjoy the rest of your round…

the mind factor

SUGGESTED READING

This is Your Brain on Sports	David Grand
Play Golf to Learn Golf	Michael Hebron
The Score Takes Care of Itself	Bill Walsh
The Inner Game of Golf	Timothy Gallwey
Extraordinary Golf	Fred Shoemaker
Attention and Motor Skill Learning	Gabrielle Wulf
The Happiness Advantage	Shawn Achor
Outliers	Malcolm Gladwell
Every Shot Must Have a Purpose	Pia Nilsson &Lynn Marriot
Perception, Cognition and Decision Training	Joan Vickers
Influence	Robert Cialdini
Wheat Belly	William Davis MD
Frogs into Princes	Richard Bandler & John Grinder

the mind factor

APPENDIX I

the mind factor

GOLF CLUBS

Has your Golf Club had the **MIND FACTOR** experience?

Over the past 10 years, Karl has presented the **MIND FACTOR** evening workshop to numerous golf clubs around the world allowing members to learn the **TOOLS** and **TECHNIQUES** used by Major Winners from around the globe. An opportunity to listen and **APPLY** the **MIND FACTOR** to their own game.

The number of **MIND FACTOR** sessions is limited every year so contact us on **www.themindfactor.com** for details of how you could make this entertaining evening a reality at **YOUR** club.

the mind factor

APPENDIX II

COACHES

Do you want to join the growing community of **MIND FACTOR COACHES** around the world?

Over 500 coaches have now taken the **MIND FACTOR** course and are certified as **MIND FACTOR** coaches. The course can be taken **EITHER** live or done in your own time online with **HOME** study.

Completion of the course gives you an in depth experience of **HOW** to get the best from both your pupils and **YOURSELF**. If you are frustrated with seeing your students improve on the range but continually fail to reach their potential on the course, then this learning experience is for you.

The "live" course only runs **ONCE** a year and **ALWAYS** sells out. If you want to look to book your place go **NOW** to **www.themindfactor.com** for details.

APPENDIX III

the mind factor

PRODUCTS

If you would like to develop your **MIND FACTOR** further we have a host of cd programmes that **SUPPORT** the learning in this book and help you reinforce your own development.

Programmes such as:

- ○ Five Shots Lower **WITHOUT** Changing Your Swing
- ○ The "Secrets to Consistency"
- ○ Mind Traps
- ○ Train your Putting Brain
- ○ Train your Golf Brain
- ○ The Players Programme
- ○ The Coaches Programme
- ○ How To Change Your Golf Swing **IMMEDIATELY**
- ○ The **MIND FACTOR** Certification Course
- ○ The **MIND FACTOR MASTER** Certification Course

All of these programmes **WILL** help you develop **YOUR MIND FACTOR** to get closer to your true potential.

Keep an eye out for new products coming soon!

Go to **www.themindfactor.com**

Lightning Source UK Ltd.
Milton Keynes UK
UKOW05f2320220414

230403UK00002B/14/P